Kids' PARTY CAKES

Kids'
PARTY
CAKES

NEW HOLLAND

Published in 2012 by
New Holland Publishers
London • Sydney • Cape Town • Auckland
www.newhollandpublishers.com

Garfield House 86–88 Edgware Road London W2 2EA United Kingdom
1/66 Gibbes Street Chatswood NSW 2067 Australia
Wembley Square First Floor Solan Road Gardens Cape Town 8001 South Africa
218 Lake Road Northcote Auckland New Zealand

A catalogue record of this book is available at the British Library and the National Library of
Australia.

ISBN: 9781742573632

Managing Director: Fiona Schultz
Publishing Director: Lliane Clarke
Designer: Stephanie Foti
Production Director: Olga Dementiev
Printer: Toppan Leefung Printing Limited

10 9 8 7 6 5 4 3 2 1

Follow New Holland Publishers on
Facebook: www.facebook.com/NewHollandPublishers

CONTENTS

Birthdays are a special time for children

—it's the one day of the year when they're guaranteed to be the centre of attention. Of course there'll be presents, but one of the highlights of the day is always the party, and the centrepiece of the party is always the cake. We have brought together an exciting range of cakes in this book that we know your kids are going to love.

INTRODUCTION

Making a memorable birthday cake doesn't have to be a chore. It will certainly take time to make the cake and then to frost and decorate it, but these easy-to-follow recipes will really simplify the whole process. Let's start with the cake.

There's no need to make a complicated cake for birthdays—the decorations are what your kids will really remember, not what was underneath. So all that's needed is a simple butter cake—easy to make and perfect for cutting and shaping. The recipes in this book call for prepared cake mix.

Using templates

For some of the more elaborate cake designs, it may be necessary to cut out your cake using a template. To make a cake using a template, see the Template section at the back of the book. Next, trace the outline onto baking paper, and cut out the shapes. Place the shapes on top of your cake, secure with toothpicks and carefully cut along the edge of the paper. Remove toothpicks and paper and assemble the cake following the directions in the recipe. Secure the individual pieces with skewers cut down to size and icing—remember to remove the skewers when you cut the cake to avoid any injuries.

If cutting fondant for your cake, use the same method but do not secure the template with toothpicks.

One of the great attractions of making a special birthday cake is the freedom you have to decorate it. As you can see by flicking through this book, almost anything can go on top of your cake, but the first step towards building your masterpiece is the frosting. Here is our tried and trusted recipe for a delicious butter cream frosting, which can then be tinted any colour you want.

Frosting

To colour butter cream frosting, you can use either icing paste or food colouring. We recommend icing paste, as it comes in a greater range of colours (so you don't have to try to mix the colour you want from two other colours) and generally provides a better result. You can find icing paste at a speciality cake decoration store.

To colour frosting, take a little icing paste, add it to your frosting and mix thoroughly with a wooden spoon. Only use a little paste at a time, as it is very concentrated—you can always add more if the colour is not strong enough.

To apply frosting to your cake, simply spread onto the cake with a palette knife. To get a smooth, flat finish (for example, for the animal faces), clean your palette knife, dip it in hot water, dry the knife, then smooth the frosting. Repeat until desired texture is reached. You will need to clean and heat the palette knife several times during this process.

To make chocolate butter cream frosting, use the following ingredients with the same method as for regular butter cream frosting.

Butter cream frosting is ideal for large surfaces, but sometimes you need to attach decorations to your cake, and for this you should use royal icing (this is the type of icing often found on Christmas and wedding cakes).

Royal icing can also be coloured in the same way as butter cream frosting.

Some recipes also call for fondant, which is a soft type of icing that's easy to roll and shape. You can buy fondant at the supermarket, where it's called white icing or rolled fondant, or from a speciality cake decoration store. Sometimes the recipe will ask you to colour the fondant—to do this, sprinkle confectioners' sugar on the work surface, add a little icing paste or food colouring, then knead the colour through the fondant until smooth. Add more colour if necessary.

royal icing

1½ cups confectioners' (icing) sugar
1 egg white
½ teaspoon lemon juice

1. Sift the confectioners' sugar.

2. Lightly beat egg white in a small bowl with a wooden spoon. Add sugar through a sieve, 1 heaped tablespoon at a time, beating well after each addition.

3. When icing reaches desired consistency, add juice and beat well.

4. Cover surface of icing tightly with cling wrap while not using to prevent crust developing. Icing will harden considerably on standing.

butter cream frosting

10½oz (300g) butter, at room temperature
2lb 12oz (1.2kg) confectioners' (icing) sugar, sieved

1. Place butter in an electric beater and beat until creamy.

2. Add sugar slowly, scraping down the sides. Beat well in between additions. If the mixture becomes too thick, add some hot water.

3. Keep adding and mixing confectioners' sugar until it has all been mixed through.

chocolate butter cream frosting

10½oz (300g) butter, at room temperature
2lb 4oz (1kg) confectioners' (icing) sugar, sieved
1 cup cocoa powder, sieved

1. Place butter in an electric beater and beat until creamy.

2. Add sugar and cocoa powder slowly, scraping down the sides. Beat well in between additions. If the mixture becomes too thick, add some hot water.

3. Keep adding and mixing until it has all been mixed through.

Now you are ready to make...

a truly spectacular birthday cake, which will make your kids the envy of all their friends and provide them with a memory they will cherish forever.

Decorations

Many of the cakes make use of a wide range of decorations, which are almost always edible. Most of the sweets we have used are readily available at your local supermarket, but for some of the special items you may have to go to a speciality sweet shop or cake decoration store. Of the inedible decorations, you can get most of them from a party supplies store or toy store, depending on the decoration, while all the flags can be made by following the templates in the Template section at the back of the book.

sour worms

jujubes

aniseed rings

jelly rings

mint leaves

red sour straps

green sour straps

jaffas

coated chocolate candy

fruit chews

mints

gum balls

Bo Peep sweets

blue sharks

mini frogs

snakes

jelly babies

jelly beans

milk bottles

strawberries and cream

coke bottles

pineapple sweets

raspberries

teeth sweets

fruit roll ups

liquorice strap

banana sweets

liquorice allsorts

cachous

chocolate sprinkles

rainbow sprinkles

edible glitter

rainbow chocolate chips

gold coins

chocolate fish

chocolate bees

mini M&M's

Giant Smarties

Smarties

Skittles

freckles

TV mix

choc-coated candy/Clinkers

liquorice bullets

star sprinkles

snow flake sprinkles

sherbet cones

ice cream cones

chocolate finger biscuits

chocolate flake bars

chocolate mint sticks

liquorice chocolate logs

red liquorice sticks

soft liquorice

sour-filled red liquorice

candy dynamite

candy cigarettes/fads

fruit sticks

musk sticks

mini musks

marshmallow puffs

round marshmallows

pink musk puffs

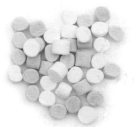

baby marshmallows

fizzles

fairy floss

chocolate cream-filled
biscuits

mini wagon wheels

CUPCAKES

Cupcakes are again all the rage, so what birthday cake book would be complete without a playful chapter of smaller cakes?

You can make all your cupcakes using one style, or mix up the decorations with a combination from different recipes. You can also make themed cupcakes as an accompaniment to a main birthday cake, allowing you to create cupcake extras at the last minute if your guest list suddenly grows.

fairy-top cupcakes

Preparation: 15 mins • Cooking: 20 mins • Makes 12

5oz (150g) butter, at room temperature

1 cup superfine (caster) sugar

3 eggs

1 teaspoon vanilla extract

½ cup milk

1½ cups self-rising (raising) flour, sifted

14oz (400g) fondant

red icing paste

royal icing (see page 9)

Cake Tin

1 x 12-cup muffin tray

Decorations

pink and white heart sprinkles

12 fairy decorations

1 Preheat oven to 320°F (160°C) and line a 12-cup muffin tray with cupcake papers.

2 Cream butter and sugar together until light and fluffy. Add eggs one at a time, beating well after each addition. Add the vanilla.

3 Add half the milk and half the flour, mix, then add the remaining milk and flour. Divide the mixture evenly between the cupcake papers.

4 Bake for 20 minutes until cooked. Cool for 5 minutes, then turn onto a cooling rack.

5 Colour 10½oz (300g) of fondant with red paste to make pink. Leave the remaining fondant plain. Spread a small amount of royal icing on top of each cupcake—this will secure the fondant.

6 On a surface dusted with confectioners' sugar, roll out pink fondant to ¹/8in (5mm) thick. Using a round cutter, cut 12 circles from the fondant. Place each circle on top of a cupcake. Roll out the plain fondant and cut with a smaller, fluted cutter. Attach together with royal icing, placing the smaller circle on top. Dot the cupcakes with royal icing to secure the hearts, then top each with fairy, see picture opposite.

twinkle twinkle cupcakes

Preparation: 15 mins • Cooking: 20 mins • Makes 12

5oz (150g) butter, at room temperature

1 cup superfine (caster) sugar

3 eggs

1 teaspoon vanilla extract

½ cup milk

1½ cups self-raising flour, sifted

10½oz (300g) fondant

black icing paste

royal icing (see page 9)

Cake Tin

1 x 12-cup muffin tray

Decorations

12 banana sweets

white and yellow star sprinkles

1 Preheat oven to 320°F (160°C) and line a 12-cup muffin tray with cupcake papers.

2 Cream butter and sugar together until light and fluffy. Add eggs one at a time, beating well after each addition. Add the vanilla.

3 Add half the milk and half the flour, mix, then add the remaining milk and flour. Divide the mixture evenly between the cupcake papers.

4 Bake for 20 minutes until cooked. Cool for 5 minutes, then turn onto a cooling rack.

5 Colour fondant black. Spread a small amount of royal icing on top of each cupcake—this will secure the fondant.

6 On a surface dusted with confectioners' sugar, roll out fondant to 1/8in (5mm) thick. Using a round cutter, cut 12 circles from the fondant. Place each circle on top of a cupcake. Dot the cupcakes with royal icing to secure the bananas and star sprinkles.

cloud-top cupcakes

Preparation: 15 mins • Cooking: 20 mins • Makes 12

5oz (150g) butter, at room temperature

1 cup superfine (caster) sugar

3 eggs

1 teaspoon vanilla extract

½ cup milk

1½ cups self-rising (raising) flour, sifted

14oz (400g) fondant

blue icing paste

royal icing (see page 9)

Cake Tin

1 x 12-cup muffin tray

Decorations

fairy floss

1 Preheat oven to 320°F (160°C) and line a 12-cup muffin tray with cupcake papers.

2 Cream butter and sugar together until light and fluffy. Add eggs one at a time, beating well after each addition. Add the vanilla.

3 Add half the milk and half the flour, mix, then add the remaining milk and flour. Divide the mixture evenly between the cupcake papers.

4 Bake for 20 minutes until cooked. Cool for 5 minutes, then turn onto a cooling rack.

5 Colour 10½oz (300g) of fondant blue, leave the remaining fondant plain. Spread a small amount of royal icing on top of each cupcake—this will secure the fondant.

6 On a surface dusted with confectioners' sugar, roll out blue fondant to ⅛in (5mm) thick. Using a round cutter, cut 12 circles from the fondant. Place each circle on top of a cupcake.

7 Roll out plain fondant and cut out birds using a small heart-shaped cutter. Attach the birds with royal icing, then place a small amount of fairy floss on top of each cupcake.

flower power cupcakes

Preparation: 15 mins • Cooking: 20 mins • Makes 12

5oz (150g) butter, at room
temperature

1 cup superfine (caster) sugar

3 eggs

1 teaspoon vanilla extract

½ cup milk

1½ cups self-rising (raising) flour,
sifted

10½oz (300g) fondant

yellow icing paste

royal icing (see page 9)

Cake Tin

1 x 12-cup muffin tray

Decorations

baby marshmallows

rainbow sprinkles

12 mint leaves

15cm (6in) piece liquorice strap,
cut into thin strips

1 Preheat oven to 320°F (160°C) and line a
12-cup muffin tray with cupcake papers.

2 Cream butter and sugar together until light
and fluffy. Add eggs one at a time, beating
well after each addition. Add the vanilla.

3 Add half the milk and half the flour, mix,
then add the remaining milk and flour.
Divide the mixture evenly between the
cupcake papers.

4 Bake for 20 minutes until cooked. Cool for
5 minutes, then turn onto a cooling rack.

5 Colour the fondant yellow. Spread a small
amount of royal icing on top of each
cupcake—this will secure the fondant.

6 On a surface dusted with confectioners'
sugar, roll out yellow fondant to ⅛in
(5mm) thick. Using a round cutter, cut
12 circles from the fondant. Place each
circle on top of a cupcake. Cut the
marshmallows in half, but keep 12 white
marshmallows whole. Dip the ends of the
whole marshmallows in royal icing then
into rainbow sprinkles. Cut mint leaves in
half horizontally, then cut out leaf shapes
with a cutter. Use royal icing to attach the
decorations in the shape of a flower.

stripes and dots cakes

Preparation: 15 mins • Cooking: 20 mins • Makes 12

5oz (150g) butter, at room temperature

1 cup superfine (caster) sugar

3 eggs

1 teaspoon vanilla extract

½ cup milk

1½ cups self-rising (raising) flour, sifted

17½oz (500g) fondant

orange icing paste

purple icing paste

green icing paste

red icing paste

royal icing (see page 9)

Cake Tin

1 x 12-cup muffin tray

1 Preheat oven to 320°F (160°C) and line a 12-cup muffin tray with cupcake papers.

2 Cream butter and sugar together until light and fluffy. Add eggs one at a time, beating well after each addition. Add the vanilla.

3 Add half the milk and half the flour, mix, then add the remaining milk and flour. Divide the mixture evenly between the cupcake papers.

4 Bake for 20 minutes until cooked. Cool for 5 minutes, then turn onto a cooling rack.

5 Colour 7oz (200g) of fondant orange, 7oz (200g) purple, 1¾oz (50g) green and 1¾oz (50g) red. Spread a small amount of royal icing on top of each cupcake—this will secure the fondant.

6 On a surface dusted with confectioners' sugar, roll out orange fondant to ⅛in (5mm) thick. Using a round cutter, cut 6 circles from the fondant. Place a circle on top of half the cupcakes. Repeat with purple fondant and remaining cupcakes.

7 Cut stripes and dots from the red and green fondant and any leftover orange and purple. Use royal icing to attach the stripes and dots.

bugs and butterflies

Preparation: 15 mins • Cooking: 20 mins • Makes 12

5oz (150g) butter, at room temperature

1 cup superfine (caster) sugar

3 eggs

1 teaspoon vanilla extract

½ cup milk

1½ cups self-raising flour, sifted

10½oz (300g) fondant

green icing paste

royal icing (see page 9)

Cake Tin

1 x 12-cup muffin tray

Decorations

jaffas

strawberries and cream

round mints, halved

Smarties

freckles

6in (15cm) piece liquorice strap, cut into thin strips

1 Preheat oven to 320°F (160°C) and line a 12-cup muffin tray with cupcake papers.

2 Cream butter and sugar together until light and fluffy. Add eggs one at a time, beating well after each addition. Add the vanilla.

3 Add half the milk and half the flour, mix, then add the remaining milk and flour. Divide the mixture evenly between the cupcake papers.

4 Bake for 20 minutes until cooked. Cool for 5 minutes, then turn onto a cooling rack.

5 Colour the fondant green. Spread a small amount of royal icing on top of each cupcake – this will secure the fondant.

6 On a surface dusted with confectioners' sugar, roll out green fondant to ⅛in (5mm) thick. Using a round cutter, cut 12 circles from the fondant. Place each circle on top of a cupcake. Use royal icing to attach the decorations in the shapes of bugs and butterflies.

buzzy bee cupcakes

Preparation: 15 mins • Cooking: 20 mins • Makes 12

5oz (150g) butter, at room
    temperature
1 cup superfine (caster) sugar
3 eggs
1 teaspoon vanilla extract
½ cup milk
1½ cups self-raising flour, sifted
10½oz (300g) fondant
green icing paste
royal icing (see page 9)

Cake Tin

1 x 12-cup muffin tray

Decorations

6 yellow, black and white
    liquorice allsorts
1 liquorice strap
12 black jelly beans

1. Preheat oven to 320°F (160°C) and line a 12-cup muffin tray with cupcake papers.

2. Cream butter and sugar together until light and fluffy. Add eggs one at a time, beating well after each addition. Add the vanilla.

3. Add half the milk and half the flour, mix, then add the remaining milk and flour. Divide the mixture evenly between the cupcake papers.

4. Bake for 20 minutes until cooked. Cool for 5 minutes, then turn onto a cooling rack.

5. Colour the fondant green. Spread a small amount of royal icing on top of each cupcake—this will secure the fondant.

6. On a surface dusted with confectioners' sugar, roll out green fondant to ⅛in (5mm) thick. Using a round cutter, cut 12 circles from the fondant. Place each circle on top of a cupcake. Cut liquorice allsorts in half crosswise. Cut out wings from the liquorice strap. Use royal icing to attach the decorations, then pipe on royal icing for the eyes.

jungle jumble cupcakes

Preparation: 15 mins • Cooking: 20 mins • Makes 12

5oz (150g) butter, at room temperature

1 cup superfine (caster) sugar

3 eggs

1 teaspoon vanilla extract

½ cup milk

1½ cups self-raising flour, sifted

10½oz (300g) fondant

green icing paste

royal icing (see page 9)

Cake Tin

1 x 12-cup muffin tray

Decorations

12 snakes

24 freckles

12 mini frogs

12 pineapple sweets

12 mint leaves

12 liquorice bullets

1 Preheat oven to 320°F (160°C) and line a 12-cup muffin tray with cupcake papers.

2 Cream butter and sugar together until light and fluffy. Add eggs one at a time, beating well after each addition. Add the vanilla.

3 Add half the milk and half the flour, mix, then add the remaining milk and flour. Divide the mixture evenly between the cupcake papers.

4 Bake for 20 minutes until cooked. Cool for 5 minutes, then turn onto a cooling rack.

5 Colour the fondant green. Spread a small amount of royal icing on top of each cupcake—this will secure the fondant.

6 On a surface dusted with confectioners' sugar, roll out fondant to ⅛in (5mm) thick. Using a round cutter, cut 12 circles from the fondant. Place each circle on top of a cupcake. Attach the decorations to each cupcake.

ladybird cupcakes

Preparation: 15 mins • Cooking: 20 mins • Makes 12

5oz (150g) butter, at room temperature

1 cup superfine (caster) sugar

3 eggs

1 teaspoon vanilla extract

½ cup milk

1½ cups self-rising (raising) flour, sifted

14oz (400g) fondant

red icing paste

black icing paste

royal icing (see page 9)

Cake Tin

1 x 12-cup muffin tray

Decorations

6in (15cm) piece liquorice strap, cut into thin strips

1   Preheat oven to 320°F (160°C) and line a 12-cup muffin tray with cupcake papers.

2   Cream butter and sugar together until light and fluffy. Add eggs one at a time, beating well after each addition. Add the vanilla.

3   Add half the milk and half the flour, mix, then add the remaining milk and flour. Divide the mixture evenly between the cupcake papers.

4   Bake for 20 minutes until cooked. Cool for 5 minutes, then turn onto a cooling rack.

5   Colour 10½oz (300g) of the fondant red, and 3½oz (100g) black. Spread a small amount of royal icing on top of each cupcake—this will secure the fondant.

6   On a surface dusted with confectioners' sugar, roll out red fondant to $^1/_8$in (5mm) thick. Using a round cutter, cut 12 circles from the fondant. Place each circle on top of a cupcake. Roll out black fondant and cut out circles and dots. Use royal icing to attach the decorations in the shape of ladybirds.

treasure-top cupcakes

Preparation: 15 mins • Cooking: 20 mins • Makes 12

5oz (150g) butter, at room
   temperature

1 cup superfine (caster) sugar

3 eggs

1 teaspoon vanilla extract

½ cup milk

1½ cups self-rising (raising) flour,
   sifted

17½oz (500g) fondant

blue icing paste

yellow icing paste

royal icing (see page 9)

Cake Tin

1 x 12-cup muffin tray

Decorations

12 chocolate gold coins

blue edible glitter

12 plastic palm trees

12 skull and crossbones flags
   (see Templates section)

1 Preheat oven to 320°F (160°C) and line a
   12-cup muffin tray with cupcake papers.

2 Cream butter and sugar together until light
   and fluffy. Add eggs one at a time, beating
   well after each addition. Add the vanilla.

3 Add half the milk and half the flour, mix,
   then add the remaining milk and flour.
   Divide the mixture evenly between the
   cupcake papers.

4 Bake for 20 minutes until cooked. Cool for
   5 minutes, then turn onto a cooling rack.

5 Colour 10½oz (300g) of the fondant blue,
   and 7oz (200g) yellow. Spread a small
   amount of royal icing on top of each
   cupcake—this will secure the fondant.

6 On a surface dusted with confectioners'
   sugar, roll out blue fondant to ⅛in (5mm)
   thick. Using a round cutter, cut 12 circles
   from the fondant. Roll out yellow fondant
   and cut out circles, then cut and discard
   crescents from the circles. Use royal icing
   to attach the yellow and blue fondant, then
   place each on top of a cupcake. Attach
   the decorations to make each cupcake a
   desert island.

ANIMAL FACES

**In this chapter all of the cakes are based on one round cake tin,
with a few extra pieces for elements such as ears.**

This means all the cakes are essentially made the same way, so after you have created one or two you will easily be able to create the rest. If you are experimenting, start with one of the simpler cakes and you will soon have the knack of putting together these friendly faces with a minimum of fuss.

bertie the bull

1 quantity butter cream frosting
  (see page 9)
brown icing paste
orange icing paste
yellow icing paste

Cake Tins

1 x 8½in (22cm) round tin
1 x No. 2 rectangular tin

Decorations

1 white baby marshmallow,
  cut in half
2 giant black Smarties
2 aniseed rings
1 white jelly ring

1 Preheat oven to 350°F (180°C) and butter and line the cake tins. Prepare 2 packets of cake mix, following directions on packet, and pour into the round cake tin. Prepare remaining 3 packets of cake mix and pour into the rectangular cake tin. Bake for 30 minutes, cover with foil and bake for another 30 minutes. Remove the round cake and bake the rectangular cake for a further 10 minutes. Test with a skewer to make sure the cakes are cooked. Leave to cool for 10 minutes, then turn onto a cooling rack.

2 While cakes cool, divide the icing in half, colour 1 half brown. Divide remaining icing in half again, colour 1 half orange and the remaining half pale yellow.

3 Use a serrated knife to level the cakes. Using the template (see Templates section), cut a section out of the round cake and discard—this is where the nose will go. Cut ear and nose from rectangular cake. Stand the nose on its end and shape the edges to fit into the round cake. Cut ear in half horizontally to make two.

4 Using a palette knife, frost the head and the outside of the ears with brown icing. Attach to the head with skewers and icing. Frost the nose and middle of ears with the orange icing. Frost the horns with the pale yellow and attach to the head.

5 Attach the marshmallow halves to the giant Smarties with icing, position on cake. Position aniseed rings and jelly ring in place. If necessary, fill a piping bag with leftover icing and seal the joins of the nose, horns and ears.

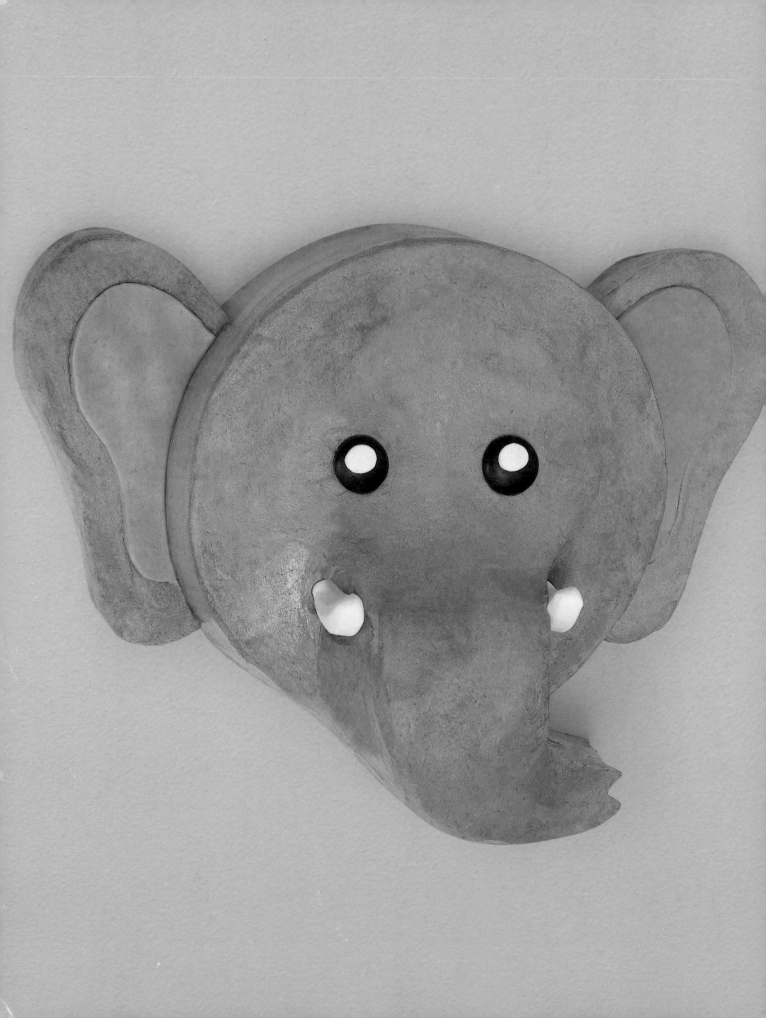

emily the elephant

6 x 12oz (340g) packets butter
cake mix

1 quantity butter cream
frosting (see page 9)

black icing paste

red icing paste

Cake Tins

1 x 8½in (22cm) round tin

1 x No. 3 rectangular tin

Decorations

1 white baby marshmallow,
cut in half

2 giant black Smarties

2 banana sweets

1 Preheat oven to 350°F (180°C) and butter
and line the cake tins.

2 Prepare 2 packets of cake mix, following
directions on packet, and pour into the round
cake tin. Prepare remaining 4 packets of cake
mix and pour into the rectangular cake tin.
Bake for 30 minutes, cover with foil and bake
for another 30 minutes. Remove the round
cake and bake the rectangular cake for a
further 15 minutes. Test with a skewer to make
sure the cakes are cooked. Leave to cool for
10 minutes, then turn onto a cooling rack.

3 While cakes cool, colour three-quarters of the
frosting light grey and the rest pink.

4 Use a serrated knife to level the cakes. Using
the template (see Templates section), cut a
section out of the round cake and discard—this
is where the trunk will go. Cut ear and trunks
from rectangular cake, then cut ear in half
horizontally to make two. Cut one trunk piece
horizontally in a curve so the trunk will look 3D.
Fit the flat trunk into the round cake, then place
the curved trunk on top.

5 Using a palette knife, frost the ears, head and
trunk grey. Frost the middle of the ear pink and
attach to the head with skewers and frosting. If
necessary, fill a piping bag with leftover frosting
and seal the joins of the ears and trunk.

6 Attach the marshmallows to the giant
Smarties with frosting, then place on cake.
Position the banana sweets as tusks.

penelope the pig

4 x 12oz (340g) packets butter
   cake mix
1 quantity butter cream frosting
   (see page 9)
red icing paste

Cake Tins

1 x 8½in (22cm) round tin
1 x No. 1 rectangular tin

Decorations

3 white baby marshmallows,
   1 cut in half
2 giant black Smarties

1   Preheat oven to 350°F (180°C) and butter and line the cake tins.

2   Prepare 2 packets of cake mix, following directions on packet, and pour into the round cake tin. Prepare remaining 2 packets of cake mix and pour into the rectangular tin. Bake for 30 minutes, cover with foil and bake for another 30 minutes. Test with a skewer to make sure the cakes are cooked. Leave to cool for 10 minutes, then turn onto a cooling rack.

3   While cakes cool, divide icing in half. Colour 1 half dark pink and the other light pink.

4   Use a serrated knife to level the cakes. Using the template (see Templates section), cut out ear and snout. Cut the ear in half horizontally to make two.

5   Using a palette knife, frost the head and ears light pink. Frost the snout and middle of the ears dark pink and attach to cake with skewers and frosting. If necessary, fill a piping bag with leftover frosting and seal the joins of the snout and ears.

6   Attach the marshmallow halves to the giant Smarties with frosting, position on cake. Attach the remaining marshmallows to the snout.

henry the hippo

5 x 12oz (340g) packets butter
  cake mix
1 quantity butter cream frosting
  (see page 9)
black icing paste
Cake Tins
1 x 8½in (22cm) round tin
1 x No. 2 rectangular tin
Decorations
1 white baby marshmallow,
  cut in half
2 giant black Smarties
2 pink musk puffs,
  ¼ cut off each
2 black jelly beans
2 milk bottles, tops cut off

1 Preheat oven to 350°F (180°C) and butter and line the cake tins.

2 Prepare 2 packets of cake mix, following directions on packet, and fill the round cake tin. Prepare remaining 3 packets of cake mix and fill the rectangular tin. Bake for 30 minutes, cover with foil and bake for another 30 minutes. Remove the round cake and bake the rectangular cake for a further 10 minutes. Test with a skewer to make sure the cakes are cooked. Leave to cool for 10 minutes, then turn onto a cooling rack.

3 While cakes cool, colour the icing grey.

4 Use a serrated knife to level the cakes. Using the template (see Templates section), cut the ear and a circle out of the rectangular cake. Cut a crescent off the circle—the crescent will be the mouth and the larger piece will be the snout. Cut the mouth in half horizontally, discard 1 half. Cut off one-third of the snout horizontally, discard. Cut the ear in half horizontally to make two.

5 Using a palette knife, frost the cake pieces, then assemble to form the face, securing with skewers and icing. Attach the marshmallow halves to the giant Smarties with icing, position on cake. Position the musk puffs on the ears, and the jelly beans and milk bottles on the snout. If necessary, fill a piping bag with leftover frosting and seal the joins of the face and ears.

gina the giraff

4 x 12oz (340g) packets butter
   cake mix
1 quantity butter cream frosting
   (see page 9)
orange icing paste
brown icing paste
red icing paste

Cake Tins

1 x 8½in (22cm) round tin
1 x No. 1 rectangular tin

Decorations

½ cup chocolate sprinkles
1 white baby marshmallow,
   cut in half
2 giant black Smarties
2 choc-covered candy (Clinkers)
2 brown Smarties

1 Preheat oven to 350°F (180°C) and butter and line the cake tins.

2 Prepare 2 packets of cake mix, following directions on packet, and pour into the round cake tin. Prepare remaining 2 packets of cake mix and fill the rectangular tin. Bake for 30 minutes, cover with foil and bake for another 30 minutes. Test with a skewer to make sure the cakes are cooked. Leave to cool for 10 minutes, then turn onto a cooling rack.

3 While cakes cool, divide frosting in half, colour 1 half orange. Divide the remaining frosting in half, colour 1 half brown and the remaining half pale pink.

4 Use a serrated knife to level the cakes. Using the template (see Templates section), cut a section out of the round cake and discard—this is where the nose will go. Cut ear and nose from rectangular cake. Stand the nose on its end and shape the edges to fit into the round cake. Cut ear in half horizontally to make two.

5 Using a palette knife, frost the head with orange. Frost the nose and ears with brown. Frost the middle of the ear with pale pink, using your finger to pat down. Attach to the head with skewers and frosting.

6 Using different-sized round cutters, mark out the dots on the giraffe, then fill each dot with the chocolate sprinkles. Attach the marshmallow halves to the giant Smarties with frosting, position on cake. Position the choc-covered candy and brown Smarties in place. If necessary, fill a piping bag with leftover frosting and seal the joins of the nose and ears.

morris the monkey

5 x 12oz (340g) packets butter cake mix

1 quantity butter cream frosting (see page 9)

black icing paste

red icing paste

royal icing (see page 9), coloured black

Cake Tins

1 x 8½in (22cm) round tin

1 x No. 2 rectangular tin

Decorations

1 white baby marshmallow, cut in half

2 giant black Smarties

2 red sour straps

1 Preheat oven to 350°F (180°C) and butter and line the cake tins.

2 Prepare 2 packets of cake mix, following directions on packet, and pour into the round cake tin. Prepare remaining 3 packets of cake mix and pour into the rectangular cake tin. Bake for 30 minutes, cover with foil and bake for another 30 minutes. Remove the round cake and bake the rectangular cake for a further 10 minutes. Test with a skewer to make sure the cakes are cooked. Leave to cool for 10 minutes, then turn onto a cooling rack.

3 While cakes cool, divide icing in half, colour 1 half dark grey and the other pink.

4 Use a serrated knife to level the cakes. Using the template (see Templates section), cut ear, mouth and eyes out of the rectangle. Cut eyes in half horizontally, discard 1 half. Cut ear in half horizontally to make two.

5 Using a palette knife, frost the round cake dark grey. Frost the mouth dark grey, apart from the top, and attach to the head. Frost the ears, eyes and top of the mouth with the pink frosting and position on the cake. If necessary, pipe any leftover frosting to seal the joins of the mouth, eyes and ears.

6 Attach the marshmallow halves to the giant Smarties with frosting, position on cake. Cut the nose from the sour straps and attach to the cake. Pipe on the mouth with royal icing.

mary the mouse

5 x 12oz (340g) packets butter
   cake mix
1 quantity butter cream
   frosting (see page 9)
orange icing paste

Cake Tins

1 x 8½in (22cm) round tin
1 x No. 2 rectangular tin

Decorations

1 white baby marshmallow,
   cut in half
2 giant black Smarties
1 musk puff
3 chocolate mint sticks,
   cut in half

1   Preheat oven to 350°F (180°C) and butter
    and line the cake tins.

2   Prepare 2 packets of cake mix, following
    directions on packet, and pour into the round
    cake tin. Prepare remaining 3 packets of cake
    mix and pour into the rectangular cake tin.
    Bake for 30 minutes, cover with foil and bake
    for another 30 minutes. Remove the round
    cake and bake the rectangular cake for a
    further 10 minutes. Test with a skewer to make
    sure the cakes are cooked. Leave to cool for
    10 minutes, then turn onto a cooling rack.

3   While cakes cool, divide the frosting in half,
    colour 1 half dark orange. Divide remaining
    frosting in half again, colour 1 half pale
    orange, leave the remaining half plain.

4   Use a serrated knife to level the cakes. Using
    the template (see Templates section), cut out
    ear and nose. Cut the ear in half horizontally
    to make two. Cut the nose in half horizontally,
    discard one half.

5   Using a palette knife, frost the middle of the
    ears pale orange. Frost the head and the
    outside of the ears dark orange. Attach to
    the cake with skewers and frosting. Frost the
    nose with the remaining plain frosting, and
    position on the cake. If necessary, fill a piping
    bag with leftover frosting and seal the joins of
    the nose and ears.

6   Attach the marshmallow halves to the giant
    Smarties with frosting, position on cake.
    Position the musk puff as the nose and the
    mint sticks as whiskers.

polly the panda

4 x 12oz (340g) packets butter
   cake mix
1 quantity butter cream frosting
   (see page 9)
black icing paste
1/3oz (10g) fondant
royal icing (see page 9),
   coloured black

Cake Tins

1 x 8½in (22cm) round tin
1 x No. 1 rectangular tin

Decorations

2 white baby marshmallows,
   cut in half
2 giant black Smarties

1 Preheat oven to 350°F (180°C) and butter
   and line the cake tins. Prepare 2 packets
   of cake mix, following directions on packet,
   and pour into the round cake tin. Prepare
   remaining 2 packets of cake mix and pour
   into the rectangular tin. Bake for 30 minutes,
   cover with foil and bake for another 30
   minutes. Test with a skewer to make sure
   the cakes are cooked. Leave to cool for 10
   minutes, then turn onto a cooling rack.

2 While cakes cool, divide the frosting in
   half. Leave one half plain. Divide remaining
   frosting in half again, colour 1 half dark
   grey and the remaining half light grey.
   Colour the fondant black and roll into an
   oval—this will be the nose.

3 Use a serrated knife to level the cakes. Using
   the template (see Templates), cut ear and
   snout from the rectangular cake. Cut the
   snout in half horizontally, discard one half.
   Cut the ear in half horizontally to make two.

4 Using a palette knife, frost the head and
   snout with plain frosting. Position the snout
   on the head. Using a 2 1/3in (6cm) round
   cutter, mark circles for the eyes, then with
   a small palette knife, scrape out the plain
   frosting and fill in with dark grey frosting.
   Frost edges of ears dark grey, frost middle of
   ears light grey.

5 Attach the ears to the head. If necessary, fill
   a piping bag with leftover frosting and seal
   the joins of the snout and ears. Attach 2
   marshmallow halves to the giant Smarties
   with icing, position onto cake. Attach 1
   marshmallow half to the side of the nose
   and position on snout. Pipe on the mouth
   with black royal icing.

zephyr the zebra

- **4 x 12oz (340g) packets butter cake mix**
- **1 quantity butter cream frosting (see page 9)**
- **black icing paste**
- **red icing paste**

Cake Tins

- **1 x 8½in (22cm) round tin**
- **1 x No. 1 rectangular tin**

Decorations

- **1 white baby marshmallow, cut in half**
- **2 giant black Smarties**
- **10 pieces soft liquorice**

1 Preheat oven to 350°F (180°C) and butter and line the cake tins.

2 Prepare 2 packets of cake mix, following directions on packet, and pour into the round cake tin. Prepare remaining 2 packets of cake mix and pour into the rectangular cake tin. Bake for 30 minutes, cover with foil and bake for another 30 minutes. Test with a skewer to make sure the cakes are cooked. Leave to cool for 10 minutes, then turn onto a cooling rack.

3 While cakes cool, divide frosting in half, leave half plain. Divide remaining frosting in half again and colour one half black and the other half pink.

4 Use a serrated knife to level the cakes. Using the template (see Templates section), cut a section out of the round cake and discard—this is where the nose will go. Cut ear, mane and nose from rectangular cake. Stand the nose on its end and shape the edges to fit into the round cake. Cut ear in half horizontally to make two.

5 Using a palette knife, frost the head with plain frosting. Frost the nose, mane and ears with black, and frost the middle of the ear with pink. Attach to the head with skewers and frosting.

6 Attach the marshmallows to the giant Smarties with icing, then place on cake. Cut 2 slices off 1 piece of liquorice and position on nose for nostrils. Roll the remaining liquorice out flat, cut out stripes and attach with frosting. If necessary, fill a piping bag with leftover frosting and seal the joins of the nose, mane and ears.

thomas the tiger

4 x 12oz (340g) packets butter
cake mix
1 quantity butter cream frosting
(see page 9), refrigerated
for 30 minutes
orange icing paste

Cake Tins

1 x 8½in (22cm) round tin
1 x No. 1 rectangular tin

Decorations

1 oval-shaped choc-covered
candy (Clinkers)
1 white baby marshmallow, cut
in half
2 giant black Smarties
10 pieces soft liquorice

1   Preheat oven to 350°F (180°C). Prepare
2 packets of cake mix, following packet
directions, and pour into the round tin.
Prepare remaining 2 packets of cake mix
and pour into the rectangular tin. Bake for 30
minutes, cover with foil and bake for another
30 minutes. Test with a skewer to make sure
the cakes are cooked. Leave to cool for 10
minutes, then turn onto a cooling rack.

2   While cakes cool, divide the frosting in half,
colour half dark orange. Divide remaining
frosting in half again, colour half light orange,
leave the remaining half plain.

3   Use a serrated knife to level the cakes. Using
the template, cut out ear and nose from
rectangular cake. Cut ear and nose in half
horizontally and discard one piece of the nose.

4   Roll out the dark orange frosting between 2
sheets of cling wrap to ¼in (1cm) thick. Make
a 8½in (22cm) circle and long rectangular
pieces for the sides, carefully place on the
cake and mould the joins together with
your hands. Cover the ears using the same
technique. Roll out the plain frosting, cover
the nose and position on the cake.

5   Using the same technique, roll out the light
orange icing. Using a 2⅓in (6cm) cutter, cut
one circle for ears. Cut in half and place onto
the ears. Using an oval cutter, cut two ovals
for the eyes. Place in position on the head.
Position the choc-covered candy on the nose.

6   Attach the marshmallow halves to the giant
Smarties with frosting, position on the ovals to
make eyes. Attach the ears to the top of the
head with skewers and frosting. If necessary,
pipe leftover frosting to seal the joins of the
nose and ears. Roll liquorice out flat, cut out
stripes and whiskers, and attach with frosting.

NUMBERS

In this chapter we have matched different themes to different ages from one up to 11, but you can create higher numbers by mixing and matching from our designs.

Some of our cakes will appeal to both boys and girls, while others are gender-specific. However, you can easily transfer a design from one cake to another, which means you'll definitely find a suitable cake, no matter what the age of your child.

number one

3 x 12oz (340g) packets butter cake mix

1 quantity butter cream frosting (see page 9)

yellow icing paste

Cake Tins

2 x No. 2 bar tins

Decorations

Smarties

Mini M&M's

Skittles

1   Preheat oven to 350°F (180°C) and butter and line the cake tins.

2   Prepare cake mix, following directions on packet, and divide between the bar tins. Bake for 30 minutes, cover with foil and bake for a further 30 minutes. Test with a skewer to make sure the cakes are cooked. Leave to cool for 10 minutes, then turn onto a cooling rack.

3   While cakes cool, colour the butter frosting yellow.

4   Use a serrated knife to level the cakes. Leave one bar cake whole and cut the remaining cake. Assemble the pieces using skewers and frosting to secure the pieces. Discard the leftover cake.

5   Using a palette knife, frost the cake, then decorate with the sweets.

number two

6 x 12oz (340g) packets butter
cake mix

1 quantity butter cream frosting
(see page 9)

Cake Tins

1 x No. 3 bar tin

1 x No. 3 rectangular tin

Decorations

marshmallow puffs

round marshmallows

baby marshmallows

fruit sticks

1 Preheat oven to 350°F (180°C) and butter
and line the cake tins.

2 Prepare 4 packets of cake mix, following
directions on packet, and pour into
rectangular cake tin. Prepare the remaining
2 packets of cake mix and pour three-
quarters into the bar tin—discard the
leftover mix.

3 Bake for 30 minutes, cover with foil and
bake for another 40 minutes. Remove the
bar cake and bake the rectangular cake for
a further 15 minutes. Test with a skewer to
make sure the cakes are cooked. Leave
to cool for 10 minutes, then turn onto a
cooling rack.

4 Use a serrated knife to level the cakes.
Cut the rectangle and bar cake using
the template (see Templates section).
Assemble the pieces to form the number
2, use skewers and frosting to secure the
pieces. Discard the leftover cake.

5 Using a palette knife, frost the cake.
Decorate with the marshmallows and fruit
sticks.

number three

- **3 x 12oz (340g) packets butter cake mix**
- **1 quantity butter cream frosting (see page 9)**
- **yellow icing paste**

Cake Tins

- **2 x 8½in (22cm) ring tins**

Decorations

- **12 yellow fruit sticks**
- **3 chocolate bees**
- **1 green snake, cut into thin strips**
- **1 orange snake, cut into thin strips**
- **1 mint leaf, halved**
- **6 blue Mini M&M's**
- **1 brown Mini M&M**

1 Preheat oven to 350°F (180°C) and butter and line the cake tins.

2 Prepare the packets of cake mix, following directions on packet, and divide between the tins. Bake for 30 minutes, cover with foil and bake for another 30 minutes. Test with a skewer to make sure the cakes are cooked. Leave to cool for 10 minutes, then turn onto a cooling rack.

3 While cakes cool, colour the butter frosting pale yellow.

4 Use a serrated knife to level the cakes, then cut the cakes as in the picture opposite. Assemble the pieces, using skewers and frosting to secure the pieces. Discard the leftover cake.

5 Using a palette knife, frost the cake. Line up 6 fruit sticks together, hold together and cut around to resemble a beehive. Repeat with remaining sticks and attach to cake. Use remaining decorations to finish the cake.

number four

4 x 12oz (340g) packets butter cake mix

1 quantity chocolate butter cream frosting (see page 9)

1 cup choc powder (Milo)

Cake Tin

1 x No. 3 rectangular tin

Decorations

8 liquorice bullets

2 orange triangle liquorice allsorts

2 orange and black liquorice allsorts

1 chocolate mint stick

1 green sour strap, cut into thin strips

1 liquorice twist, sliced into 8

2 yellow and black liquorice allsorts

1 chocolate flake bar, broken

1 Preheat oven to 350°F (180°C) and butter and line the cake tin. Prepare packets of cake mix, following directions on packet, and pour into cake tin. Bake for 50 minutes, reduce oven temperature to 320°F (160°C), cover with foil and bake for another 25 minutes. Test with a skewer to make sure the cake is cooked. Leave to cool for 10 minutes, then turn onto a cooling rack.

2 Use a serrated knife to level the cake. Using the template (see Template section), cut the cake, see picture 1. Assemble the pieces to form the number 4, using skewers and icing to secure the pieces. Discard the leftover cake.

3 Using a palette knife, frost the cake. Cut a 1in-wide (2.5cm), curved piece of paper and place on the cake—this will be the bulldozer's track. Sift choc powder liberally over the cake then remove the paper. Spoon choc powder at the top of the cake to resemble a pile of dirt. Add the liquorice bullets and triangle allsorts.

4 To assemble the crane, cut one of the orange allsorts in half. Attach to the top of the whole orange allsort with leftover frosting. Cut a groove into the front, insert the mint stick and lay over a strip of sour strap. Attach 4 slices of liquorice twist as wheels.

5 To assemble the bulldozer, place a yellow allsort at the end of the bulldozer track. Cut the other yellow allsort in half horizontally and place in front. Attach remaining liquorice twists as wheels. Pile the flake in front.

number five

4 x 12oz (340g) packets butter cake mix

1 quantity butter cream frosting (see page 9)

orange icing paste

royal icing (see page 9), coloured black

Cake Tins

1 x No. 3 bar tin

1 x 8½in (22cm) ring tin

Decorations

4 pieces soft liquorice

3 snakes, different colours

Smarties

1. Preheat oven to 350°F (180°C) and butter and line the cake tins.

2. Prepare 2 packets of cake mix, following directions on packet, and pour into the bar tin. Prepare remaining 2 packets of cake mix and three-quarter-fill the ring tin—discard the leftover mix. Bake for 30 minutes, cover with foil and bake for another 30 minutes. Remove the ring cake and bake the bar cake for a further 10 minutes. Test with a skewer to make sure the cakes are cooked. Leave to cool for 10 minutes, then turn onto a cooling rack.

3. While cakes cool, colour the butter frosting orange.

4. Use a serrated knife to level the cakes, then cut the cakes. Assemble the pieces to make the number 5, using skewers and frosting to secure the pieces. Discard the leftover cake.

5. Using a palette knife, frost the cake. Roll out the liquorice and cut into thin strips to form the ladder. Use the remaining decorations to finish the cake.

number six

4 x 12oz (340g) packets butter
cake mix

1 quantity butter cream frosting
(see page 9)

red icing paste

royal icing (see page 9), half plain
and half coloured green

Cake Tins

1 x No. 3 bar tin

1 x 8½in (22cm) ring tin

Decorations

1 piece soft liquorice

1 pink jelly bean, halved

1 purple jelly bean, halved

2 pink diamond jubes,
cut in half horizontally

2 purple round jubes,
cut in half horizontally

1 pink round jube,
cut in half horizontally

white baby marshmallows, halved

pink baby marshmallows, halved

Bo Peep sweets

1. Preheat oven to 350°F (180°C) and butter and line the cake tins.

2. Prepare 2 packets of cake mix, following directions on packet, and pour into the bar tin. Prepare remaining 2 packets of cake mix and three-quarter-fill the ring tin—discard the leftover mix. Bake for 30 minutes, cover with foil and bake for another 30 minutes. Remove the ring cake and bake the bar cake for a further 10 minutes. Test with a skewer to make sure the cakes are cooked. Leave to cool for 10 minutes, then turn onto a cooling rack.

3. While cakes cool, colour the butter frosting pale pink.

4. Use a serrated knife to level the cakes, then cut the cakes using the template (see Templates section). Assemble the pieces, using skewers and frosting to secure the pieces. Discard the leftover cake.

5. Using a palette knife, frost the cake, then decorate. Roll the liquorice flat, cut into thin strips and use as bodies for the butterflies. Fill a piping bag with green royal icing and pipe on the leaves of the flowers. Pipe the plain royal icing into the centre of the flowers.

number seven

4 x 12oz (340g) packets butter
cake mix

1 quantity butter cream frosting
(see page 9)

blue icing paste

7oz (200g) fondant

red icing paste

purple icing paste

orange icing paste

Cake Tins

2 x No. 3 bar tins

1 x 12-cup muffin tray

Decorations

1 small ice cream cone

white fairy floss

1 Preheat oven to 350°F (180°C) and butter and line the bar tins. Place 3 cupcake cases in the muffin tray.

2 Prepare the cake mix, following directions on packet. Three-quarter-fill the 3 cupcake cases, then divide remaining cake mix between the bar tins. Bake for 20 minutes. Test the cupcakes with a skewer to make sure they are done, then remove from the oven. Cover the bar cakes with foil and bake for another 50 minutes. Test with a skewer to make sure the cakes are cooked. Leave to cool for 10 minutes, then turn onto a cooling rack.

3 Meanwhile, colour the frosting bright blue. Divide the fondant into quarters and colour one quarter red, one purple, one orange, and leave the remaining fondant plain.

4 Use a serrated knife to level the cakes. Cut the bar cakes as in the picture opposite. Assemble the pieces to form the number 7, using skewers and frosting to attach the pieces. Discard the leftover cake.

5 Using a palette knife, frost the cake. Cut 3 sections from the ice cream cone for baskets. Cut the tops off the cupcakes and cut into a balloon shape. Discard the cupcake bottoms.

6 On a surface dusted with confectioners' sugar, roll out the red fondant to 1/8in (5mm) thick and use it to cover one balloon. Repeat with the purple and orange fondant. Cut strips from the remaining coloured fondant and place onto each balloon. Attach balloons to cake and add baskets. Roll out plain fondant, cut out birds, then attach fairy floss.

number eight

3 x 12oz (340g) packets butter cake mix

1 quantity butter cream frosting (see page 9)

green icing paste

3½oz (100g) fondant

black icing paste

½ cup desiccated coconut

Cake Tins

2 x 8½in (22cm) ring tins

Decorations

3 pieces soft liquorice, 2 cut in half lengthwise, 1 left whole

1 red Skittle

1 yellow Skittle

1 green Skittle

2 red sour straps, cut in half lengthwise

4 toy racing cars

1 chequered flag (see Templates section)

1 Preheat oven to 350°F (180°C) and butter and line the cake tins. Prepare packets of cake mix, following directions on packet, and divide between tins. Bake for 30 minutes, cover with foil and bake for another 30 minutes. Test with a skewer to make sure the cakes are cooked. Leave to cool for 10 minutes, then turn onto a cooling rack.

2 While the cakes cool, colour the butter icing green and the fondant grey. Place the coconut in either a bowl or plastic bag and mix through green paste a little at a time to achieve desired colour.

3 Use a serrated knife to level the cakes. Slice off a fraction of each ring cake so that they join up neatly, as in the picture opposite. Assemble the pieces, using skewers and icing to secure the pieces.

4 Using a palette knife, frost the cake. On a surface dusted with confectioners' sugar, roll out the fondant to ⅛in (5mm) thick, place the template on top and cut out, then carefully lay on top of the cake and smooth down.

5 Sprinkle the coconut around the outside of the cake. Roll the whole piece of liquorice flat, cut out 3 holes the size of Skittles and press the Skittles into the holes to make a traffic light, then position on the cake. Cut the halved pieces of liquorice into thirds. Cut sour straps in half lengthwise, attach 3 pieces of liquorice to each sour strap with leftover frosting and position on cake as barriers. Add the cars and chequered flag.

number nine

4 x 12oz (340g) packets butter cake mix

1 quantity butter cream frosting (see page 9)

red icing paste

black icing paste

3½oz (100g) fondant

Cake Tins

1 x No. 3 bar tin

1 x 8½in (22cm) ring tin

Decorations

2 white jelly beans

1 pair disposable chopsticks

2 blue sour straps, cut into strips

musk pills

blue cachous

silver cachous

1 Preheat oven to 350°F (180°C) and butter and line the cake tins.

2 Prepare 2 packets of cake mix, following directions on packet, and pour into the bar tin. Prepare remaining 2 packets of cake mix and three-quarter-fill the ring tin—discard the leftover mix. Bake for 30 minutes, cover with foil and bake for another 30 minutes. Remove the ring cake and bake the bar cake for a further 10 minutes. Test with a skewer to make sure the cakes are cooked. Leave to cool for 10 minutes, then turn onto a cooling rack.

3 While cakes cool, divide the butter frosting in half, colour one half red and the other black.

4 Use a serrated knife to level the cakes, then cut the cakes using the template (see Templates section). Assemble the pieces, using skewers and frosting to secure the pieces. Discard the leftover cake.

5 Using a palette knife, frost the straight piece of cake black and the outside of the ring cake red. On a surface dusted with confectioners' sugar, roll out the fondant to ⅛in (5mm) thick, place the template on top and cut out, then carefully lay on top of the cake and smooth down.

6 Using a round cutter, remove the centre of the fondant and line the inside of the round cake with the remaining fondant. Attach the jelly beans to the ends of the chopsticks. Use the remaining decorations to finish the cake.

number ten

8 x 12oz (340g) packets butter cake mix

2 quantities butter cream frosting (see page 9)

yellow icing paste

blue icing paste

¼ cup desiccated coconut

1 teaspoon choc powder (Milo)

Cake Tins

1 x 8½in (22cm) ring tin

1 x No. 2 rectangular tin

2 x No. 2 bar tins

Decorations

1 red jelly bean

1 red sour strap, cut into thin strips

2 hundreds and thousands liquorice allsorts

1 roll up

3 pineapple sweets

2 sherbet cones

2 coke bottles

2 blue sharks

soccer ball candle

rainbow chocolate candy

1 cocktail umbrella

1 Preheat oven to 350°F (180°C) and butter and line the cake tins. Prepare 2 packets of cake mix, following directions on packet, and three-quarter-fill the ring tin—discard leftover mix. Prepare 3 packets of cake mix and pour into the rectangular tin. Bake for 30 minutes, cover with foil and bake for another 30 minutes. Remove the ring cake and bake the rectangular cake for 10 minutes more. Test cakes with a skewer. Leave to cool for 10 minutes, then turn onto a cooling rack.

3 Prepare the remaining 3 packets of cake mix and divide between the bar tins. Bake for 30 minutes, cover with foil and bake for a further 30 minutes. Test with a skewer to make sure the cakes are cooked. Leave cakes to cool for 10 minutes, then turn onto a cooling rack.

4 Meanwhile, colour 1 quantity of butter frosting yellow. Colour three-quarters of the remaining frosting blue. Divide the final quarter of frosting in half, colour half dark blue and leave the rest plain.

5 Cut the cakes as in picture 1 (see page 82). Assemble the pieces as in picture 2 (see page 83), using skewers and frosting to secure the pieces.

6 Add some yellow paste to the coconut. Add choc powder and mix. Frost the number 1 yellow and the number 0 blue. Use the dark blue and plain frosting for waves.

7 Make crabs from jelly beans and sour straps. Make octopuses from allsorts and sour straps. Cut edges of the roll up to resemble a towel. Cut 4 wedges from 1 pineapple and arrange around the other 2 pineapples to make fish. Cut ends off the sherbet cones to make sandcastles.

number eleven

6 x 12oz (340g) packets butter cake mix

1 quantity butter cream frosting (see page 9)

black icing paste

13oz (380g) fondant

red icing paste

blue icing paste

green icing paste

Cake Tins

2 x No. 2 bar tins

Decorations

1 piece soft liquorice

2 teeth sweets

2 candy cigarettes/fads, cut into small pieces

1   Preheat oven to 350°F (180°C) and butter and line the cake tins.

2   Prepare 3 packets of cake mix, following directions on packet, and divide between the bar tins. Bake for 30 minutes, cover with foil and bake for a further 30 minutes. Test with a skewer to test they're done. Leave to cool for 10 minutes, then turn onto a cooling rack. Repeat with the remaining 3 packets of mix—you will now have 4 bar cakes.

3   While the cakes cool, colour the frosting dark grey. Colour 5oz (150g) of the fondant red, 5oz (150g) pink, $^2/_3$oz (20g) blue, $^2/_3$oz (20g) green, and leave the remaining 1½oz (40g) plain.

4   Use a serrated knife to level the cakes. Leave 2 whole and cut the remaining 2 as in picture 1 (see page 86).

5   Take the top pieces of the cake and cut a horizontal wedge in the top left corner of one and the top right corner of the other, see picture 1. Attach the pieces to form two number 1s, using skewers and frosting to secure the pieces.

6   Using a palette knife, frost the cakes. Make the frosting thicker at the top for the eyes. Using the red fondant, mould 2 tongues, then shape 4 lips and attach to the top and bottom of each mouth. Press the teeth into the top and position the fads in the bottom of each mouth. Use the pink, blue, green and plain fondant to make the eyes and attach to the cakes as in picture 2 (page 87).

Picture 1

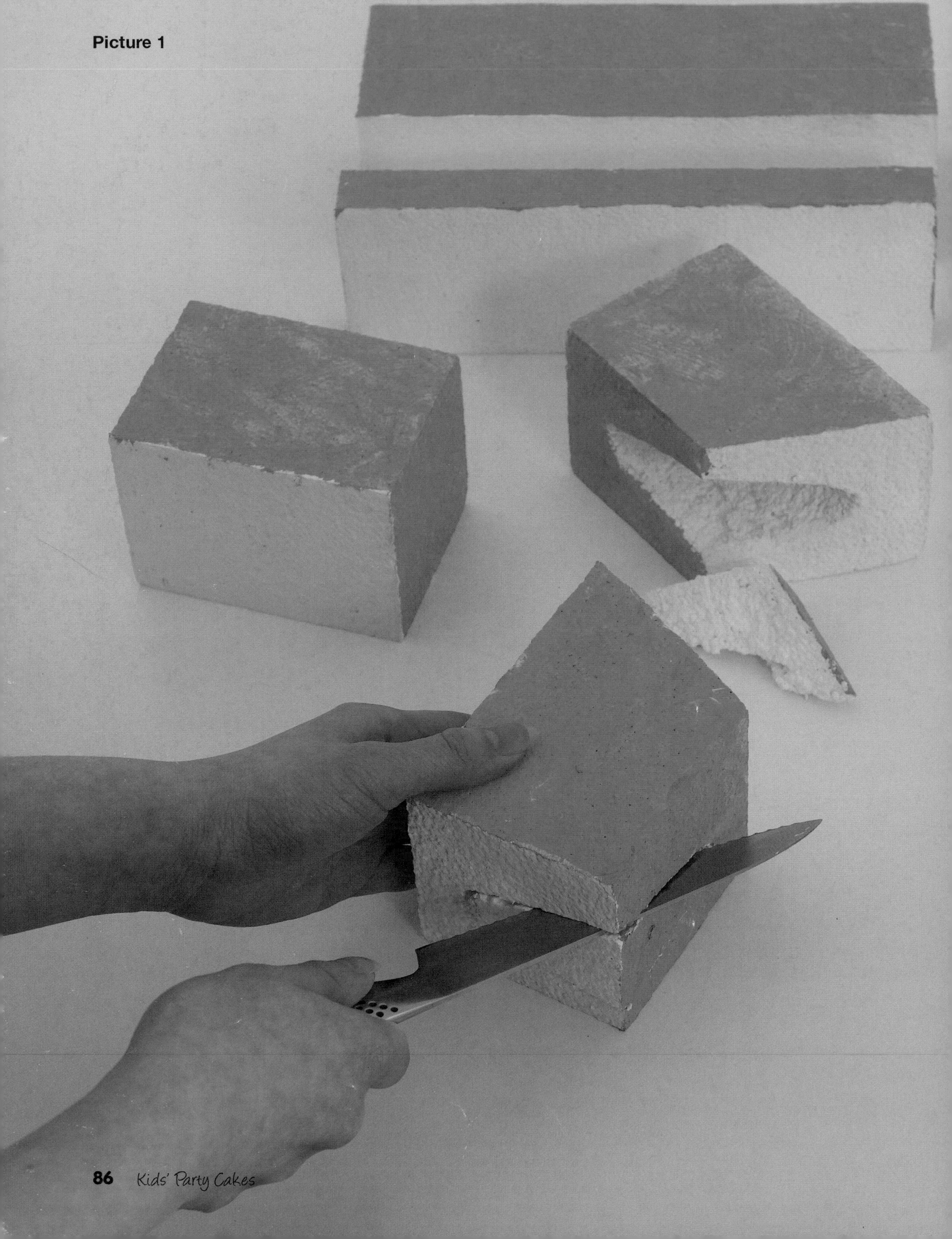

DOMES

In this chapter there is a mixture of easy and slightly more advanced cakes, based around only two different cake tins.

We have deliberately limited the use of cake tins so you don't have to end up with a cupboard full of baking tins that only come out once per year. There is also a range of different topping and decorating techniques, so you can prepare a fairy princess as easily as you can a mountain with dirt bikes on it.

princess clara

2 x 12oz (340g) packets butter cake mix

1 quantity butter cream frosting (see page 9)

purple icing paste

Cake Tin

1 x large Dolly Varden tin

Decorations

purple ribbon

1 doll, legs removed

Bo Peep sweets

diamond jubes, cut in half

oval jubes, cut in half

mini musks

musk sticks, sliced

pink baby marshmallows, cut in half

1 Preheat oven to 350°F (180°C) and butter and line the cake tin.

2 Prepare packets of cake mix, following directions on packet, and pour into the cake tin. Bake for 30 minutes, cover with foil and bake for another 30 minutes. Test with a skewer to make sure the cake is cooked. Leave to cool for 10 minutes, then turn onto a cooling rack.

3 While cake cools, colour the butter frosting purple.

4 Use a serrated knife to level the bottom of the cake. Using a palette knife, frost the cake purple. Wrap ribbon around doll to make her halter top. Place the doll on top of cake and decorate.

princess taylor

2 x 12oz (340g) packets butter cake mix

¼ quantity butter cream frosting (see page 9)

blue icing paste

1lb 9oz (700g) fondant

Cake Tin

1 x large Dolly Varden tin

Decorations

ribbon

1 doll, legs removed

1 Preheat oven to 350°F (180°C) and butter and line the cake tin.

2 Prepare packets of cake mix, following directions on packet, and pour into the cake tin. Bake for 30 minutes, cover with foil and bake for another 30 minutes. Test with a skewer to make sure the cake is cooked. Leave to cool for 10 minutes, then turn onto a cooling rack.

3 While the cake cools, colour the frosting blue, then colour 17½oz (500g) of fondant blue. Wrap the ribbon around the doll to make her halter top.

4 Use a serrated knife to level the bottom of the cake. Frost the cake with the blue frosting—this is for the fondant to stick to.

5 On a surface dusted with confectioners' sugar, roll out the blue fondant to ⅛in (5mm) thick, then lay over the cake. Place doll on top of cake. Roll out the plain fondant in a semi-circle and cut out shapes. Place over the blue fondant.

princess maggie

2 x 12oz (340g) packets butter cake mix

1 quantity butter cream frosting (see page 9)

yellow icing paste

8½oz (240g) fondant

blue icing paste

orange icing paste

purple icing paste

Cake Tin

1 x large Dolly Varden tin

Decorations

8 fruit sticks

fruit chews

1 doll, legs removed

1 Preheat oven to 350°F (180°C) and butter and line the cake tin.

2 Prepare packets of cake mix, following directions on packet, and pour into the cake tin. Bake for 30 minutes, cover with foil and bake for another 30 minutes. Test with a skewer to make sure the cake is cooked. Leave to cool for 10 minutes, then turn onto a cooling rack.

3 While cake cools, colour the butter frosting pale yellow. Divide the fondant into three portions and colour one portion blue, one orange and one purple.

4 Use a serrated knife to level the bottom of the cake. Using a palette knife, frost the cake yellow and decorate.

5 On a surface dusted with confectioners' sugar, roll out the purple and orange fondant to ⅛in (5mm) thick. Using different-sized star cutters, cut out stars to decorate the cake. Roll out the blue fondant and make the doll's top and bow and place on top of cake.

princess vivian

2 x 12oz (340g) packets butter cake mix

17½oz (500g) fondant

½ quantity butter cream frosting (see page 9)

red icing paste

purple icing paste

yellow icing paste

green icing paste

Cake Tin

1 x large Dolly Varden tin

Decorations

red ribbon

1 doll, legs removed

1 Preheat oven to 350°F (180°C) and butter and line the cake tin.

2 Prepare packets of cake mix, following directions on packet, and pour into the cake tin. Bake for 30 minutes, cover with foil and bake for another 30 minutes. Test with a skewer to make sure the cake is cooked. Leave to cool for 10 minutes, then turn onto a cooling rack.

3 While cake cools, colour the fondant red. Divide the butter cream frosting into 5, leave one-fifth plain and colour each of the other four-fifths with one of the coloured pastes. Wrap the ribbon around the doll to make her halter top.

4 Use a serrated knife to level the bottom of the cake. Using a palette knife, frost the cake with the plain frosting—this is for the fondant to stick to.

5 On a surface dusted with confectioners' sugar, roll out the fondant to 1/8in (5mm) thick, then lay over the cake. Fill piping bags with the coloured frosting and pipe flowers onto the fondant. Place doll on top of cake.

snowy mountain

2 x 12oz (340g) packets butter cake mix

1 quantity chocolate butter cream icing (see page 9)

5oz (150g) white fondant

royal icing (see page 9)

½ cup confectioners' (icing) sugar

Cake Tin

1 x large Dolly Varden tin

Decorations

1 orange liquorice allsort

1 marshmallow puff

rainbow chocolate chips

9in (15cm) piece liquorice strap

5oz (150g) white chocolate

2 snowballs

¼ cup desiccated coconut

white gumballs

round mints

white snowflake sprinkles

1 Preheat oven to 350°F (180°C) and butter and line the cake tin.

2 Prepare packets of cake mix, following directions on packet, and pour into the cake tin. Bake for 30 minutes, cover with foil and bake for another 30 minutes. Test with a skewer to make sure the cake is cooked. Leave to cool for 10 minutes, then turn onto a cooling rack.

3 Use a serrated knife to level the bottom of the cake. Using a palette knife, frost the cake with the chocolate icing. Roll out fondant on baking paper and cut out the 'snow cap'. Place on top of the cake.

4 To make the nose, cut a small triangle from the orange piece of the liquorice allsort and attach to the marshmallow puff with royal icing. Attach the rainbow chocolate chips as mouth and eyes, also using royal icing. Make the hat out of the liquorice strap.

5 Place a bowl over a saucepan of simmering water. Add chocolate and stir until melted. Quickly coat snowballs with chocolate and sprinkle over coconut. (If your party is around Christmas time, you can simply buy white snowballs.)

6 Thread a skewer through the middle of the snowballs, head and hat and attach to the top of the cake. Decorate with the remaining decorations and dust liberally with confectioners' sugar.

dirt bike

2 x 12oz (340g) packets butter cake mix

1 quantity chocolate butter cream frosting (see page 9)

1 cup choc powder (Milo)

Cake Tins

1 x large Dolly Varden tin

1 x 12-cup muffin tray

Decorations

TV mix

3 plastic pine trees

2 plastic 4-wheeler dirt bikes

1 finish line banner (see Templates section)

1 chequered flag (see Templates section)

1 Preheat oven to 350°F (180°C). Butter and line the cake tin with baking paper, and line 2 muffin cups with cupcake cases.

2 Prepare packets of cake mix, following directions on packet. Three-quarter-fill the 2 cupcake cases. Pour the remainder of the cake mix into the Dolly Varden tin. Bake for 20 minutes. Test the cupcakes with a skewer to make sure they are done, then remove from the oven. Cover the Dolly Varden cake with foil and bake for another 40 minutes. Test with a skewer to make sure the cake is cooked. Leave to cool for 10 minutes, then turn onto a cooling rack.

3 Use a serrated knife to level the bottom of the cake. Using a palette knife, frost the cake with the chocolate frosting.

4 Cut the cupcakes in half, then cut and discard a curved section out of each so they will sit flush with the cake. Attach the cupcake halves to the cake using skewers and frosting. Frost the cupcake pieces with chocolate frosting, then dust the whole cake liberally with the chocolate powder. Place the TV mix in piles around the cake, then position the pine trees, bikes, finish line and flag.

witches' brew

2 x 12oz (340g) packets butter cake mix

1 packet green jelly

¼ quantity butter cream frosting (see page 9)

red icing paste

⅓oz (10g) fondant

1 quantity chocolate butter cream frosting (see page 9)

Cake Tin

1 x large Dolly Varden tin

Decorations

1 packet liquorice chocolate logs

5 red liquorice sticks

1 chocolate flake bar, broken

1 marshmallow puff

1 brown Smartie

4in (10cm) piece liquorice strap

2 brown peanut M&M's

2 red mini frogs

4 sour worms

2 teeth sweets

1 Preheat oven to 350°F (180°C) and butter and line the cake tin.

2 Prepare packets of cake mix, following directions on packet, and pour into the cake tin. Bake for 30 minutes, cover with foil and bake for another 30 minutes. Test with a skewer to make sure the cake is cooked. Leave to cool for 10 minutes, then turn onto a cooling rack.

3 Meanwhile, prepare the jelly following directions on packet and refrigerate to set.

4 While cakes cool, colour the butter frosting red and colour the fondant pale pink.

5 Hollow out the top third of the cake. Using a palette knife, frost the cake with the chocolate icing. Spread the red frosting onto the base of the cake.

6 Arrange the liquorice logs, red liquorice sticks and flake bar at the base to resemble logs. Spoon the jelly into the cake. Mould the fondant to look like a hand. Attach the marshmallow to the Smartie with icing to make an eye. Use liquorice and M&M's to make spiders. Add remaining decorations to jelly.

Stencil outlines are an easy way to create a fun theme for birthday cake decorations.

Simply cut out the shape and frost as directed—this gives you a flat surface to work on for the decorations, making it easy to create wonderfully themed cakes that look spectacular. We have provided a range of cakes that will suit either girls or boys, and which is sure to keep them enchanted year after year.

dinosaur

6 x 12oz (340g) packets butter cake mix

1 quantity butter cream frosting (see page 9)

green icing paste

1 cup sugar

Cake Tin

1 x No. 4 rectangular tin

Decorations

1 liquorice strap, cut into thin strips

1 strawberry cream

6 mini musks

1 brown Smartie

1 Preheat oven to 350°F (180°C) and butter and line the cake tin.

2 Prepare cake mix, following directions on packet, and pour into the cake tin. Bake for 60 minutes, reduce oven temperature to 320°F (160°C), cover with foil and bake for another 40 minutes. Test with a skewer to make sure the cake is cooked. Leave to cool for 10 minutes, then turn onto a cooling rack.

3 While cake cools, colour the frosting green. Place the sugar in either a bowl or plastic bag and mix through the paste, a little at a time, to achieve desired colour.

4 Use a serrated knife to level the cake. Using the template (see Template section), cut out the shapes from the cake. Assemble the pieces to form the dinosaur and use skewers and frosting to secure the pieces. Discard the leftover cake.

5 Using a palette knife, frost the cake. Sprinkle the coloured sugar over the cake. Cut the red part from the strawberry cream and attach the Smartie to the white part with frosting, then place on the head. Attach the mini musks as toes.

6 Carefully place liquorice along outline of the cake. Use a small paintbrush to remove any excess sugar from the liquorice.

seahorse

6 x 12oz (340g) packets butter cake mix

1½ quantities chocolate butter cream frosting (see page 9)

brown icing paste

1 cup sugar

Cake Tin

1 x No. 4 rectangular tin

Decorations

1 liquorice strap, cut into thin strips

1 blue Skittle

1 marshmallow, halved

6 sour worms, halved

1 Preheat oven to 350°F (180°C) and butter and line the cake tin.

2 Prepare cake mix, following directions on packet, and pour into the cake tin. Bake for 60 minutes, reduce oven temperature to 320°F (160°C), cover with foil and bake for another 40 minutes. Test with a skewer to make sure the cake is cooked. Leave to cool for 10 minutes, then turn onto a cooling rack.

3 While cake cools, place the sugar in either a bowl or plastic bag and mix through the paste, a little at a time, to achieve desired colour.

4 Use a serrated knife to level the cake. Using the template (see Templates section), cut out the shapes from the cake. Assemble the pieces to form the seahorse and use skewers and frosting to secure the pieces. Discard the leftover cake.

5 Using a palette knife, frost the cake. Sprinkle the coloured sugar over the cake. Carefully place liquorice along outline of the cake. Use a small paintbrush to remove any excess sugar from the liquorice. Attach the Skittle to a marshmallow half with frosting and place on the head. Discard the blue worm halves and place the red halves on the fin.

train

6 x 12oz (340g) packets butter
cake mix

1 quantity butter cream frosting
(see page 9)

black icing paste

1 cup sugar

blue icing paste

Cake Tin

1 x No. 4 rectangular tin

Decorations

1 liquorice strap,
cut into thin strips

2 red sour straps,
cut into strips

1 Preheat oven to 350°F (180°C) and butter
and line the cake tin.

2 Prepare cake mix, following directions on
packet, and pour into the cake tin. Bake
for 60 minutes, reduce oven temperature
to 320°F (160°C), cover with foil and bake
for another 40 minutes. Test with a skewer
to make sure the cake is cooked. Leave
to cool for 10 minutes, then turn onto a
cooling rack.

3 While cake cools, colour the frosting black.
Divide the sugar in half. Place each half
in either bowls or plastic bags and, using
the icing paste, colour one light blue and
one black. Add a little at a time, to achieve
desired colours.

4 Use a serrated knife to level the cake.
Using the template (see Templates
section), cut out the shapes from the cake.
Using a palette knife, frost the cake blue.
Sprinkle the coloured sugar over the cake
as in picture opposite. Carefully place
liquorice along outline of the cake. Use a
small paintbrush to remove any excess
sugar from the liquorice. Complete the
decoration with the sour straps.

horse

6 x 12oz (340g) packets butter
cake mix

1 cup sugar

2 tablespoons cocoa powder

1 quantity chocolate butter
cream frosting (see page 9)

Cake Tin

1 x No. 4 rectangular tin

Decorations

1 liquorice strap,
cut into thin strips

2 aniseed rings

1¾oz (50g) fondant

blue icing paste

royal icing (see page 9)

1 Preheat oven to 350°F (180°C) and butter
and line the cake tin.

2 Prepare cake mix, following directions on
packet, and pour into the cake tin. Bake
for 60 minutes, reduce oven temperature
to 320°F (160°C), cover with foil and bake
for another 40 minutes. Test with a skewer
to make sure the cake is cooked. Leave
to cool for 10 minutes, then turn onto a
cooling rack.

3 While the cake cools, place the sugar
in either a bowl or plastic bag and mix
through the cocoa.

4 Use a serrated knife to level the cake.
Using the template (see Templates
section), cut out the shapes from the cake.
Assemble the pieces to form the horse and
use skewers and frosting to secure the
pieces. Discard the leftover cake.

5 Using a palette knife, frost the cake.
Sprinkle the coloured sugar over the cake.
Carefully place liquorice along outline of the
cake. Use liquorice and the aniseed rings
to make the bridle. Use a small paintbrush
to remove any excess sugar from the
liquorice.

6 Colour the fondant with the blue paste,
then roll out to ⅛in (5mm) thick. Use the
fondant and royal icing to make the first
place ribbon.

moon

4 x 12oz (340g) packets butter
  cake mix

1/2 quantity butter cream frosting
  (see page 9)

black icing paste

Cake Tin

1 x No. 3 rectangular tin

Decorations

edible glitter

1 liquorice strap,
  cut into thin strips

1 choc-covered candy (Clinkers)

1 Preheat oven to 350°F (180°C) and butter
   and line the cake tin.

2 Prepare cake mix, following directions on
   packet, and pour into the cake tin. Bake
   for 50 minutes, cover with foil and bake
   for another 25 minutes. Test with a skewer
   to make sure the cake is cooked. Leave
   to cool for 10 minutes, then turn onto a
   cooling rack.

3 While cake cools, colour the frosting grey.

4 Use a serrated knife to level the cake.
   Using the template (see Templates
   section), cut out the shapes from the cake.
   Discard the leftover cake.

5 Using a palette knife, frost the cake.
   Sprinkle the glitter over the cake. Carefully
   place liquorice along outline of the cake,
   then make the mouth, eye and eyelashes.
   Use a small paintbrush to remove any
   excess sugar from the liquorice. Place the
   choc-covered candy in the middle of the
   eye.

teddy bear

6 x 12oz (340g) packets butter
  cake mix

1 quantity butter cream frosting
  (see page 9)

orange icing paste

1 cup sugar

yellow icing paste

Cake Tin

1 x No. 4 rectangular tin

Decorations

1 liquorice strap

1 Preheat oven to 350°F (180°C) and butter and line the cake tin.

2 Prepare cake mix, following directions on packet, and pour into the cake tin. Bake for 60 minutes, reduce oven temperature to 320°F (160°C), cover with foil and bake for another 40 minutes. Test with a skewer to make sure the cake is cooked. Leave to cool for 10 minutes, then turn onto a cooling rack.

3 While cake cools, colour the frosting orange. Reserve 2 tablespoons of sugar, then place the remaining sugar in either a bowl or plastic bag and mix through the orange paste, a little at a time, to achieve desired colour. Using the same technique, colour the 2 tablespoons yellow.

4 Use a serrated knife to level the cake. Using the template (see Templates section), cut out the shapes from the cake. Assemble the pieces to form the teddy bear and use skewers and frosting to secure the pieces. Discard the leftover cake.

5 Using a palette knife, frost the cake. Sprinkle the orange sugar over the cake. Cut long, thin strips from the liquorice strap and carefully place along outline of the cake, then make the snout. Use a small paintbrush to remove any excess sugar from the liquorice. Sprinkle yellow sugar over the snout and cut a circle of liquorice for the nose and two tiny pieces for eyes.

kite

6 x 12oz (340g) packets butter cake mix

1 quantity butter cream icing (see page 9)

orange icing paste

red icing paste

1 cup sugar

Cake Tin

1 x No. 4 rectangular tin

Decorations

1 liquorice strap, cut into thin strips

2 red sour straps, cut into thin strips

1 Preheat oven to 350°F (180°C) and butter and line the cake tin.

2 Prepare cake mix, following directions on packet, and pour into the cake tin. Bake for 60 minutes, reduce oven temperature to 320°F (160°C), cover with foil and bake for another 40 minutes. Test with a skewer to make sure the cake is cooked. Leave to cool for 10 minutes, then turn onto a cooling rack.

3 While cake cools, divide butter frosting in half. Colour one half orange and the other half red. Divide the sugar in half, place each half in either bowls or plastic bags and, using the icing paste, colour one orange and one red. Add a little at a time, to achieve desired colours.

4 Use a serrated knife to level the cake. Using the template (see Templates section), cut out the shapes from the cake. Assemble the pieces to form the kite and use skewers and icing to secure the pieces. Discard the leftover cake. Cut the tail pieces in half horizontally.

5 Using a palette knife, frost the cake red and orange. Sprinkle the coloured sugar over the cake. Carefully place liquorice along outline of the cake, including the tail pieces, and between the red and orange sections. Use a small paintbrush to remove any excess sugar from the liquorice. Use liquorice and the strips of sour strap to complete the decoration.

sleeping cat

4 x 12oz (340g) packets butter cake mix

½ quantity butter cream frosting (see page 9)

black icing paste

1 cup sugar

royal icing (see page 9), coloured black

Cake Tin

1 x No. 3 rectangular tin

Decorations

1 liquorice strap, cut into thin strips

1 pink jube, halved

1 Preheat oven to 350°F (180°C) and butter and line the cake tin.

2 Prepare cake mix, following directions on packet, and pour into the cake tin. Bake for 50 minutes, reduce oven temperature to 320°F (160°C), cover with foil and bake for another 25 minutes. Test with a skewer to make sure the cake is cooked. Leave to cool for 10 minutes, then turn onto a cooling rack.

3 While cake cools, colour the icing dark grey. Place the sugar in either a bowl or plastic bag and mix through the paste, a little at a time, to achieve desired colour.

4 Use a serrated knife to level the cake. Using the template (see Templates section), cut out the shapes from the cake. Using a palette knife, frost the cake. Carefully place liquorice along outline of the cake. Sprinkle the coloured sugar over the cake. Use a small paintbrush to remove any excess sugar from the liquorice. Pipe the royal icing onto the cat to make whiskers, eyes, ears etc, and position the jube for the nose.

love duck

6 x 12oz (340g) packets butter cake mix

1 quantity butter cream frosting (see page 9)

yellow icing paste

orange icing paste or food colouring

1 cup sugar

Cake Tin

1 x No. 4 rectangular tin

Decorations

1 liquorice strap

1 Preheat oven to 350°F (180°C) and butter and line the cake tin.

2 Prepare cake mix, following directions on packet, and pour into the cake tin. Bake for 60 minutes, reduce oven temperature to 320°F (160°C), cover with foil and bake for another 40 minutes. Test with a skewer to make sure the cake is cooked. Leave to cool for 10 minutes, then turn onto a cooling rack.

3 While cake cools, colour the frosting yellow. Reserve 2 tablespoons of sugar, then place the remaining sugar in either a bowl or plastic bag and mix through the yellow paste or food colouring, a little at a time, to achieve desired colour. Using the same technique, colour the 2 reserved tablespoons orange.

4 Use a serrated knife to level the cake. Using the template (see Template section), cut out the shapes from the cake. Using a palette knife, frost the cake yellow. Sprinkle the yellow sugar over the cake. Cut long, thin strips from the liquorice strap and carefully place along outline of the cake, then make the wing and beak. Use a small paintbrush to remove any excess sugar from the liquorice. Sprinkle orange sugar over the beak, and cut an oval of liquorice for the eye.

ADVANCED CAKES

For the more ambitious or for those with some experience at baking, this chapter mixes together an array of themes and ideas that start from fairly easy cakes and move through to the more complicated.

These cakes will really knock the socks off everyone at the party, but don't be put off if they seem too complicated at first—all it takes is a little perseverance and you'll be baking like a master in no time.

happy star

6 x 12oz (340g) packets butter cake mix

1 quantity butter cream frosting (see page 9)

yellow icing paste

1 tablespoon sugar

red icing paste

1½oz (40g) fondant

black icing paste

royal icing (see page 9), coloured black

Cake Tin

1 x 11¾in (30cm) square tin

Decoration

2in (5cm) piece liquorice strap, cut into strips

1 Preheat oven to 350°F (180°C) and butter and line the cake tin.

2 Prepare packets of cake mix, following directions on packet, and pour into the cake tin. Bake for 30 minutes, cover with foil and bake for another 30 minutes. Test with a skewer to make sure the cake is cooked. Leave to cool for 10 minutes, then turn onto a cooling rack.

3 While cake cools, colour the frosting yellow and the sugar red. Colour 1oz (30g) of fondant black, leave the remaining fondant plain.

4 Use a serrated knife to level the cake, then round the edges. Using the template (see Templates section), cut out shapes from cake and discard the leftover cake. Using a palette knife, frost the cake yellow.

5 On a surface dusted with confectioners' sugar, roll out black fondant. Cut out 2 ovals and shape into eyes. Use plain fondant for pupils. Pipe on smile and nose with royal icing. Sprinkle on the red sugar for cheeks. Attach the liquorice as eyebrows.

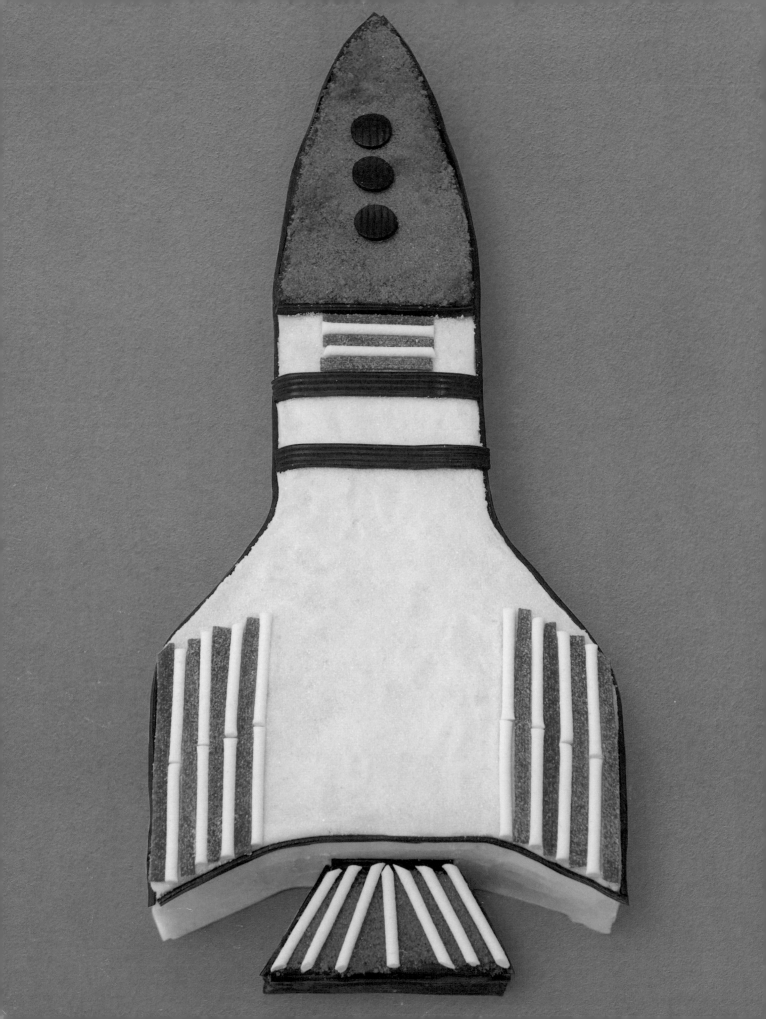

rocket

6 x 12oz (340g) packets butter
   cake mix

1½ quantities butter cream
   frosting (see page 9)

yellow icing paste

red icing paste

1 cup sugar

Cake Tin

1 x No. 4 rectangular tin

Decorations

1 liquorice strap

blue sour straps, cut into strips

fads

1 Preheat oven to 350°F (180°C) and butter
   and line the cake tin.

2 Prepare cake mix, following directions on
   packet, and pour into the cake tin. Bake
   for 60 minutes, reduce oven temperature
   to 320°F (160°C), cover with foil and bake
   for another 40 minutes. Test with a skewer
   to make sure the cake is cooked. Leave
   to cool for 10 minutes, then turn onto a
   cooling rack.

3 While cake cools, colour one quantity
   of frosting yellow and the remaining half
   quantity red. Divide the sugar in half. Place
   each half in either bowls or plastic bags
   and, using the icing paste, colour one
   yellow and one red. Add a little at a time,
   to achieve desired colours.

4 Use a serrated knife to level the cake.
   Using the template (see Templates
   section), cut out the shapes from the cake.
   Discard the leftover cake. Cut the tail in
   half horizontally and discard 1 half.

5 Using a palette knife, frost the centre piece
   of the cake yellow. Frost the tip and tail
   red. Attach the tip and the tail to the cake
   with skewers and icing.

6 Cut long, thin strips and three circles from the
   liquorice strap. Carefully place strips along
   outline of the cake as in picture opposite.
   Sprinkle the coloured sugar over the cake.
   Use a small paintbrush to remove any excess
   sugar from the liquorice. Use liquorice, sour
   straps and fads to decorate cake.

mermaid

6 x 12oz (340g) packets butter cake mix

1 quantity butter cream frosting (see page 9)

blue icing paste

yellow icing paste

9oz (250g) fondant

purple icing paste

1 tablespoon coconut, toasted

royal icing (see page 9), coloured red

Cake Tins

1 x No. 3 rectangular tin

1 x large Dolly Varden tin

Decorations

1 doll

1 green sour strap

1 green jelly bean

6 chocolate shells, halved

4 foiled chocolate fish

1 Preheat oven to 350°F (180°C) and butter and line the cake tins.

2 Prepare 2 packets of cake mix, following directions on packet, and pour into the Dolly Varden tin. Prepare remaining 4 packets of cake mix and pour into the rectangular tin. Bake for 30 minutes, cover with foil and bake for another 30 minutes. Remove the Dolly Varden cake and bake the rectangular cake for a further 15 minutes. Test with a skewer to make sure the cakes are cooked. Leave to cool for 10 minutes, then turn onto a cooling rack.

3 While cakes cool, colour half the butter cream frosting blue. Remove 2–3 tablespoons and colour dark blue. Colour remaining frosting yellow.

4 Colour 7oz (200g) of fondant purple, leaving remaining fondant plain. Roll out the purple fondant to 1/8in (5mm) thick and wrap around the doll's legs as in picture. Roll out plain fondant and, using the template (see Templates section), cut out the tail. Attach to the feet of the doll. Pipe the royal icing onto the tail.

5 Use a serrated knife to level the cakes. Using a palette knife, frost the rectangular cake blue, then use the dark blue frosting to make waves. Frost the Dolly Varden cake yellow and attach to the rectangular cake with skewers.

6 Use the sour strap and jelly bean to make the crab. Attach the shells to the yellow cake and place the fish on the blue cake. Sit the mermaid on top of the yellow cake.

volcano island

6 x 12oz (340g) packets butter cake mix

1 quantity butter cream frosting (see page 9)

green icing paste

red icing paste

orange icing paste

½ cup desiccated coconut

½ quantity chocolate butter cream frosting (see page 9)

¼ cup choc powder (Milo)

Cake Tins

1 x No. 3 rectangular tin

1 x large Dolly Varden tin

Decorations

2 red sour straps

TV mix

3 plastic palm trees

4 plastic lizards

1 Preheat oven to 350°F (180°C) and butter and line the cake tins.

2 Prepare 2 packets of cake mix, following directions on packet, and pour into the Dolly Varden tin. Prepare remaining 4 packets of cake mix and pour into the rectangular tin. Bake for 30 minutes, cover with foil and bake for another 30 minutes. Remove the Dolly Varden cake and bake the rectangular cake for a further 15 minutes. Test with a skewer to make sure the cakes are cooked. Leave to cool for 10 minutes, then turn onto a cooling rack.

3 While cakes cool, colour half the butter cream frosting green. Divide the remaining butter cream frosting in half again, colour half red and half orange. Place the coconut in either a bowl or plastic bag and mix through green paste, a little at a time, to achieve desired colour.

4 Use a serrated knife to level the cakes. Using a palette knife, frost the rectangular cake green, then sprinkle over the coconut. Frost the Dolly Varden cake with chocolate frosting and attach to the rectangular cake with skewers. Dust liberally with choc powder, then frost the top of the cake with red and orange icing.

5 Cut the sour straps into thin strips and attach to the top of volcano. Place the TV mix, palm tress and lizards on the rectangular cake.

treasure island

6 x 12oz (340g) packets butter cake mix

1 quantity butter cream frosting (see page 9)

blue icing paste

yellow icing paste

Cake Tins

1 x No. 3 rectangular tin

1 x large Dolly Varden tin

Decorations

11¾in (30cm) piece liquorice strap

1 red sour strap

1 red jelly bean

blue and green rainbow chocolate chips

chocolate coins

3 plastic palm trees

1 skull and crossbones flag (see Templates section)

1 Preheat oven to 350°F (180°C) and butter and line the cake tins.

2 Prepare 2 packets of cake mix, following directions on packet, and pour into the Dolly Varden tin. Prepare remaining 4 packets of cake mix and pour into the rectangular tin. Bake for 30 minutes, cover with foil and bake for another 30 minutes. Remove the Dolly Varden cake and bake the rectangular cake for a further 15 minutes. Test with a skewer to make sure the cakes are cooked. Leave to cool for 10 minutes, then turn onto a cooling rack.

3 While cakes cool, colour half the butter cream frosting blue. Remove 2–3 tablespoons and colour dark blue. Colour remaining frosting yellow.

4 Use a serrated knife to level the cakes. Using a palette knife, frost the rectangular cake blue, then use the dark blue frosting to make waves. Frost the Dolly Varden cake yellow and attach to the rectangular cake with skewers.

5 Cut the liquorice strap to make shark fins. Use the sour strap and jelly bean to make the crab. Place the chocolate chips, coins, palm trees and flag on the cake.

campfire

- **2 x 12oz (340g) packets butter cake mix**
- **½ quantity butter cream frosting (see page 9)**
- **red icing paste**
- **orange icing paste**
- **2 x 17½oz (500g) chocolate Swiss rolls**
- **½ quantity chocolate butter cream frostings (see page 9)**
- **3 x 17½oz (500g) lamington Swiss rolls**

Cake Tin

- **1 x large Dolly Varden tin**

1. Preheat oven to 350°F (180°C) and butter and line the cake tin.

2. Prepare packets of cake mix, following directions on packet, and pour into the cake tin. Bake for 30 minutes, cover with foil and bake for another 30 minutes. Test with a skewer to make sure the cake is cooked. Leave to cool for 10 minutes, then turn onto a cooling rack.

3. While cake cools, colour three-quarters of the butter frosting red, and the remaining quarter orange.

4. Cut the cake to resemble a flame. Using a palette knife, frost the cake with the red icing and small amounts of orange. Frost the chocolate Swiss rolls with chocolate frosting.

5. Assemble the cakes to resemble a campfire. If necessary, use skewers to secure.

birthday pizza

2 x 12oz (340g) packets butter
   cake mix
1 teaspoon cocoa powder
¼ cup desiccated coconut
yellow icing paste
7oz (200g) fondant
½ cup strawberry jam

Cake Tin

1 x 8½in (22cm) round tin

Decorations

black jelly beans
green jelly babies, sliced
   lengthwise
coke bottles, sliced lengthwise

1 Preheat oven to 350°F (180°C) and butter and line the cake tin.

2 Prepare packets of cake mix, following directions on packet, and pour into the cake tin. Bake for 30 minutes, cover with foil and bake for another 30 minutes. Test with a skewer to make sure the cake is cooked. Leave to cool for 10 minutes, then turn onto a cooling rack.

3 While cake cools, mix cocoa with one tablespoon of hot water. Mix coconut in a bowl with a small amount of yellow paste and 1 teaspoon of water.

4 Use a serrated knife to level the cake. On a surface dusted with confectioners' sugar, roll out the fondant into a long rectangle. Spread a little jam around the sides of the cake—this will help the fondant stick to the cake—then attach the fondant to the cake.

5 Spread remaining jam on top of the cake to resemble tomato sauce. With a small paintbrush, lightly brush on the cocoa mix to resemble pastry. Sprinkle on the coconut and the decorations.

elmo the blue heeler

4 x 12oz (340g) packets butter cake mix

1 quantity butter cream frosting (see page 9)

blue icing paste

12oz (350g) fondant

black icing paste

orange icing paste

red icing paste

royal icing (see page 9), coloured black

Cake Tin

1 x No. 3 rectangular tin

1 Preheat oven to 350°F (180°C) and butter and line the cake tin.

2 Prepare packets of cake mix, following directions on packet, and pour into the cake tin. Bake for 50 minutes, cover with foil and bake for another 25 minutes. Test with a skewer to make sure the cake is cooked. Leave to cool for 10 minutes, then turn onto a cooling rack.

3 While cake cools, colour the frosting dark blue.

4 Colour 7oz (200g) of fondant black, ¾oz (25g) orange, $1/3$oz (10g) pink, and leave the remaining fondant plain.

5 Use a serrated knife to level the cake. Use the template (see Templates section) to cut out the pieces of cake. Attach the ears to the cake with skewers and frosting.

6 Using a palette knife, frost the cake. Pipe the royal icing on to make the smile. On a surface dusted with confectioners' sugar, roll out the fondant to $1/8$in (5mm) thick, then cut out using the template. Position the fondant on the cake.

caravan

3 x 12oz (340g) packets butter cake mix

½ quantity butter cream frosting (see page 9)

blue icing paste

Cake Tins

1 x 8½in (22cm) round tin

1 x 12-cup muffin tray

Decorations

2 mini wagon wheels

1 liquorice strap, cut into thin strips

2 sour-filled red liquorice

1 hundreds and thousands liquorice allsort

3 green sour straps

4 raspberries

1 blue sour strap

2 orange Skittles

1 Preheat oven to 350°F (180°C) and butter and line the cake tin with baking paper, and line 2 muffin cups with cupcake cases.

2 Prepare packets of cake mix, following directions on packet. Three-quarter-fill the 2 cupcake cases. Pour the remainder of the cake mix into the round tin. Bake for 20 minutes. Test the cupcakes with a skewer to make sure they are done, then remove from oven. Cover the round cake with foil and bake for another 40 minutes. Test with a skewer to make sure the cake is cooked. Leave to cool for 10 minutes, then turn onto a cooling rack.

3 While cakes cool, colour the frosting blue.

4 Use a serrated knife to level the cake. Using a ruler, mark the centre of the cake and cut in half. Attach the cake halves together side by side using skewers and icing.

5 Using a palette knife, frost the cake. Cut the muffins in half and place underneath the cake, see picture 1 (page 144). Attach the wagon wheels to cake, see picture 2 (page 144). Carefully place the liquorice along outline of the cake, then use it to make the windows, sunroof and door. Make the towbar from red liquorice and the allsort. Use the remaining decorations to make the tail lights and curtains.

Picture 1

Picture 2

butterfly

6 x 12oz (340g) packets butter cake mix

1 quantity butter cream frosting (see page 9)

orange icing paste

red icing paste

Cake Tin

1 x No. 4 rectangular tin

Decorations

1 piece soft liquorice

1 liquorice strap

purple, blue and black edible glitter

1 Preheat oven to 350°F (180°C) and butter and line the cake tin.

2 Prepare cake mix, following directions on packet, and pour into the cake tin. Bake for 60 minutes, reduce oven temperature to 320°F (160°C), cover with foil and bake for another 40 minutes. Test with a skewer to make sure the cake is cooked. Leave to cool for 10 minutes, then turn onto a cooling rack.

3 While cake cools, colour three-quarters of the frosting orange and one-quarter red.

4 Use a serrated knife to level the cake. Using the template (see Templates section), cut out the shapes from the cake. Cut the small wing in half horizontally, then assemble the pieces to form the small butterfly, securing with skewers and icing. Discard the leftover cake. Cut a section out of the large wing to give the body definition, see picture 3 (page 145).

5 Using a palette knife, frost the cakes orange. Place the soft liquorice in the centre of the small butterfly for the body. Cut the liquorice strap and place down the centre of the large body. Pipe red frosting around the outside of the butterflies' wings and pipe shapes in the middle. Fill these shapes using the edible glitter. Use strips of liquorice for the feelers.

buzzy bee

4 x 12oz (340g) packets butter cake mix

1½ quantities butter cream icing (see page 9)

red icing paste

yellow icing paste

9oz (250g) fondant

black icing paste

Cake Tins

1 x 8¾in (22cm) round tin

1 x 6in (15cm) round tin

1 x 5in (12.5cm) round tin

Decoration

craft wire

1 Preheat oven to 350°F (180°C) and butter and line the cake tins. Prepare 2 packets of cake mix, following packet directions, and pour into the 8¾in (22cm) cake tin. Prepare 1 packet of cake mix and pour into the 6in (15cm) tin. Prepare remaining packet of cake mix and pour half into the 5in (12.5cm) tin.

2 Bake the cakes for 30 minutes, cover with foil and bake for another 30 minutes. Test with a skewer to make sure the cakes are cooked. Leave to cool for 10 minutes, then turn onto a cooling rack.

3 Meanwhile, divide butter frosting into thirds, colour one-third red, one-third yellow, and leave the remaining third plain. Colour 3½oz (100g) fondant red, 3½oz (100g) black, ¾oz (25g) yellow, and leave the rest plain.

4 Use a serrated knife to level the cakes, then cut the smallest cake in half horizontally.

5 Using a palette knife, frost the 8¾in (22cm) cake red, the 6in (15cm) cake plain, and both halves of the 5in (12.5cm) cake yellow. Assemble together to form the bee, securing with skewers, and seal the joins with frosting.

6 On a surface dusted with confectioners' sugar, roll out the black and plain fondant. Using the template (see Templates section), cut the pieces of the bee's face and position on cake. Roll the red fondant into solid balls and attach to the end of skewers that have been wrapped in craft wire, then attach to the head. Roll a 2in-long (5cm) cylinder of yellow fondant, cut in half and place one half on each wing. Use the remaining black and yellow fondant for the stripes.

astronaut on the moon

2 x 12oz (340g) packets butter
   cake mix
1lb 12oz (800g) fondant
black icing paste
¼ cup sugar
blue icing paste
¼ quantity butter cream frosting
   (see page 9)
Cake Tin
1 x 8½in (22cm) round tin
Decorations
1 flag (see Templates section)

1. Preheat oven to 350°F (180°C) and butter and line the cake tin. Prepare packets of cake mix, following directions on packet, and pour into the cake tin. Bake for 30 minutes, cover with foil and bake for another 30 minutes. Test with a skewer to make sure the cake is cooked. Leave to cool for 10 minutes, then turn onto a cooling rack.

3. While cake cools, colour 1lb 5oz (600g) of fondant grey, leaving 7oz (200g) plain. Colour sugar blue.

4. Use a serrated knife to level the cake, then frost with butter cream frosting—this will help the fondant stick to the cake. On a surface dusted with confectioners' sugar, roll out fondant to ⅛in (5mm) thick. Place over the cake, gently smooth onto cake and trim.

5. Using different-shaped circles, push depressions into the cake to make craters using different sized round chocolate. Using the leftover grey fondant, roll into different size balls and position on cake as rocks.

6. To make the astronaut, roll the plain fondant into balls—3 large balls for the body and helmet, 10 smaller ones for the legs and 6 for the arms. Squash them together to make the astronaut. Shape two hands and attach to the ends of the arms. Flatten a ball and place on top of the body, then position the helmet on top. Roll 2 small balls for the side of the helmet, then 2 smaller balls, also for the side of the helmet.

7. Dilute a small amount of blue paste with hot water. Using a small paintbrush, paint on the visor. Position the astronaut on the cake with the flag and sprinkle over the coloured sugar.

bookworm

4 x 12oz (340g) packets butter cake mix

2lb 4oz (1kg) fondant

purple icing paste

green icing paste

¼ quantity butter cream frosting (see page 9)

1 teaspoon instant coffee

royal icing (see page 9), coloured black

Cake Tin

1 x No. 3 rectangular tin

1 Preheat oven to 350°F (180°C) and butter and line the cake tin.

2 Prepare packets of cake mix, following directions on packet, and pour into the cake tin. Bake for 30 minutes, cover with foil and bake for another 45 minutes. Test with a skewer to make sure the cake is cooked. Leave to cool for 10 minutes, then turn onto a cooling rack.

3 While cake cools, colour 1lb 5oz (600g) of fondant purple, 7oz (200g) pale green, and leave the remainder plain.

4 Use a serrated knife to level the cake. Using a palette knife, frost the cake with the butter cream frosting—this will help the fondant stick to the cake.

5 On a bench dusted with confectioners' sugar, roll out the purple fondant to ¹/₈in (5mm) thick, then lay over the cake. Roll a long strip of plain fondant approximately 2¾in (7cm) wide and 27½in (70cm) long. Carefully wrap around the edge of the cake, then make horizontal marks on the fondant so it resembles pages. Mix the coffee with 1 tablespoon hot water, brush on to pages.

6 Roll out about 15 balls of green fondant, then stick together to make the 2 halves of the worm. Cut out circles of purple fondant then cut as in the picture opposite. Place the cut circles on the cake, then position the 2 worm halves. Pipe wording onto the cake with the royal icing.

kenny the truck

4 x 12oz (340g) packets butter cake mix

1 quantity butter cream frosting (see page 9)

blue icing paste

black icing paste

Cake Tins

2 x No. 1 rectangular tins

Decorations

3 packets mini wagon wheels

1 liquorice strap, cut into thin strips

5 blue sour straps, 1 cut in half

orange Smarties

orange Skittles

2 sour-filled red liquorice

liquorice bullets

4 chocolate liquorice logs

4 jaffas

1 Preheat oven to 350°F (180°C) and butter and line the cake tins.

2 Prepare 2 packets of cake mix, following directions on packet, and fill 1 cake tin. Prepare remaining 2 packets of cake mix and fill the other tin. Bake for 30 minutes, cover with foil and bake for another 30 minutes. Test with a skewer to make sure the cakes are cooked. Leave to cool for 10 mins, then turn onto a cooling rack.

3 While cakes cool, colour half the butter frosting blue. Divide remaining frosting in half, colour half grey and leave the remaining half plain.

4 Use a serrated knife to level the cakes. Cut 1 cake in half horizontally and round the top corners of one half, see picture 1 (page 156). Attach the front of the cake together with skewers and frosting as in picture 1.

5 Using a palette knife, frost the front of the cake blue and the back grey. Using the plain frosting, attach wagon wheels to the underside of the cake—this will lift the cake, see picture 2 (page 157). Attach wagon wheels to the side of the cake for wheels. Outline the doors and windows with liquorice. Use the remaining decorations to finish the rest of the truck.

toy robot

6 x 12oz (340g) packets butter
cake mix

1 quantity butter cream frosting
(see page 9)

black icing paste

Cake Tin

1 x No. 4 rectangular tin

Decorations

2 red sour straps

1 green sour strap

1 liquorice strap

4 pieces soft red liquorice

2 round liquorice allsorts

green fizzles

white fizzles

4 raspberries

2 aniseed rings

yellow jelly beans

white jelly beans

royal icing

1 Preheat oven to 350°F (180°C) and butter and line the cake tin.

2 Prepare packets of cake mix, following directions on packet, and pour into the cake tin. Bake for 60 minutes, cover with foil and bake for another 40 minutes. Test with a skewer to make sure the cake is cooked. Leave to cool for 10 minutes, then turn onto a cooling rack.

3 While cake cools, colour the frosting grey.

4 Use a serrated knife to level the cake. Using the template (see Templates section), cut out the pieces of cake. Cut pieces 3 and 4 in half horizontally.

5 Using a palette knife, ice all the pieces grey—use a skewer to hold them while icing. Assemble the pieces, using the skewers to secure them together. Place pieces 1 and 2 side by side to make the body. Pieces 3 and 4 are the legs and arms. Piece 5 is the head and pieces 6 and 7 are the feet.

6 Using a small, round cutter, cut circles out of the sour straps and attach to the cake. Use the remaining decorations to finish the rest of the robot.

dorothy the dinosaur

2 x 12oz (340g) packets butter
  cake mix
1 x 17½oz (500g) jam roll
1lb 12oz (800g) fondant
green icing paste
yellow icing paste
black icing paste
½ quantity butter cream frosting
  (see page 9)
Cake Tin
1 x 8½in (22cm) round tin

1 Preheat oven to 350°F (180°C) and butter and line the cake tin. Prepare packets of cake mix, following directions on packet, and pour into the cake tin. Bake for 30 minutes, cover with foil and bake for another 30 minutes. Test with a skewer to make sure the cake is cooked. Leave to cool for 10 minutes, then turn onto a cooling rack.

2 While cake cools, colour 1lb 5oz (600g) of fondant green, 3½oz (100g) yellow, 1¾oz (50g) black, and leave the rest plain.

3 Use a serrated knife to level the cake. Using a ruler, mark the centre of the cake and cut in half. Attach the cake halves together side by side using skewers and frosting.

4 Cut the jam roll in half on an angle, see picture 1. Round the end of 1 half for the head. Cut the sides off the remaining piece—this will be the tail, see picture 2. Attach the pieces together to make the dinosaur using skewers and frosting. Using a palette knife, frost the cake—this will help the fondant stick to the cake.

5 On a surface dusted with confectioners' sugar, roll out the green fondant. Place this over the cakes, smooth over carefully with your hands and trim. Shape the tail with your hands. Roll out the black and plain fondant. Using the template (see Template section), cut out the teeth. Cut out eyes, then attach eyes and teeth to the head with frosting.

6 Using the leftover green fondant, mould 4 feet and attach with frosting. Make spikes and attach with frosting. Roll different-sized balls of yellow fondant and flatten, then attach with frosting as scales.

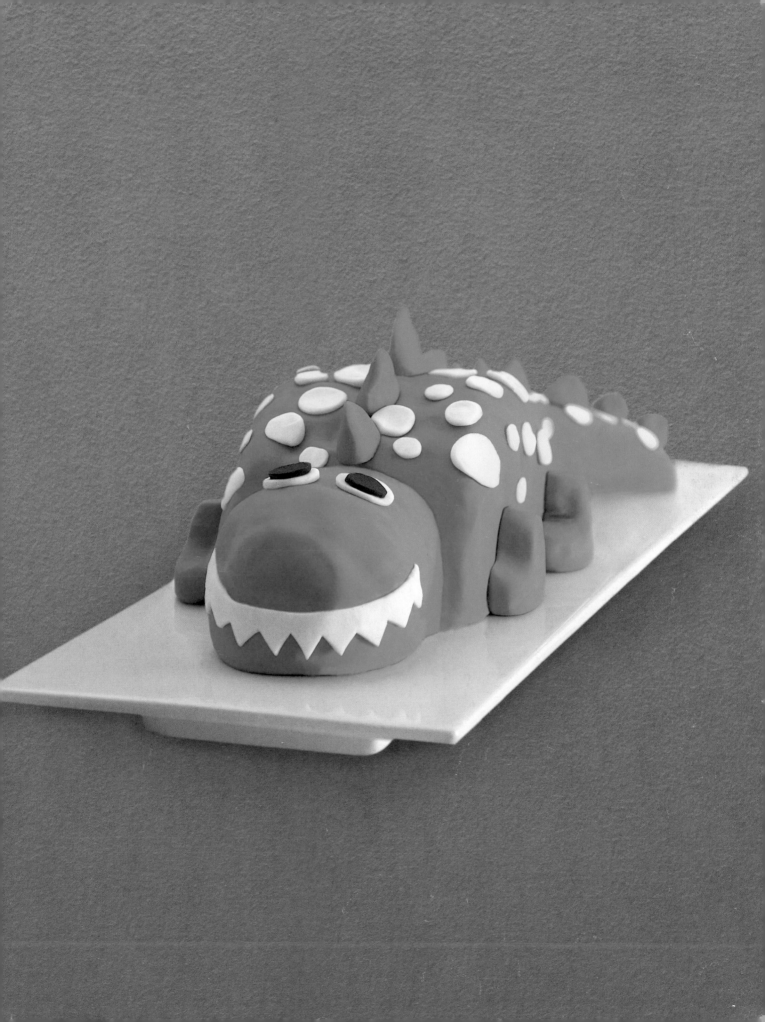

magic castle

13 x 12oz (340g) packets butter cake mix

2½ quantities butter cream frosting (see page 9)

black icing paste

blue icing paste

1¾oz (50g) fondant

Cake Tins

1 x No. 2 rectangular tin

1 x No. 3 rectangular tin

1 x No. 4 rectangular tin

Decorations

7 ice cream cones

Smarties

6 flags (see Templates section)

choc-covered candy (Clinkers)

1 Preheat oven to 350°F (180°C) and butter and line the cake tins.

2 Prepare 3 packets of cake mix, following directions on packet, and pour into the No. 2 rectangular tin. Prepare 4 packets of cake mix and pour into the No. 3 tin. Bake the cakes for 35 minutes, cover with foil and bake for another 40 minutes. Test with a skewer to make sure the cakes are cooked. Leave to cool for 10 minutes, then turn onto a cooling rack.

3 Prepare 6 packets of cake mix, following directions on packet, and pour into the No. 4 tin. Bake for 60 minutes, reduce oven temperature to 320°F (160°C), cover with foil and bake for another 40 minutes. Test with a skewer to make sure the cake is cooked. Leave to cool for 10 minutes, then turn onto a cooling rack.

4 While cakes cool, colour 2 quantities of butter frosting grey. Colour the remaining half quantity blue. Colour fondant blue.

5 Use a serrated knife to level the cakes. Using the template (see Templates section), cut the largest cake.

6 Using a palette knife, frost the pieces of cake—use a skewer to hold them while icing. Assemble the pieces, using the skewers to secure them together. The No. 3 rectangular cake will be the base, then place the No. 2 rectangular cake in the centre. Position piece number 5 from the No. 4 rectangular cake on top. Stand pieces 1 and 3 on the back of the base, and stand pieces 2 and 4 on either side of the base, at the front. Secure all the pieces with frosting and skewers.

7 Carefully cut the tops off the ice cream cones with a serrated knife and set aside. Frost the bottom of 5 cones with blue frosting, attach to the top of the 4 towers and place 1 in the centre of the castle. Using a piping bag with a small star nozzle, pipe around the bottom of the cones. Cut the reserved tops of the cones in half, attach 6 halves to the cake—these will be the balconies. Pipe with blue frosting.

8 On a surface dusted with confectioners' sugar, roll out fondant to 1/8in (5mm) thick. Using the template, cut out the windows, then attach to the towers and pipe the outline with frosting. Place 4 Smarties underneath each window. Cut the remaining 2 ice cream cones in half lengthwise, and use these and the remaining decorations to finish the rest of the castle.

summer holiday

4 x 12oz (340g) packets butter cake mix

1 packet blue jelly

½ quantity butter cream frosting (see page 9)

orange icing paste

Cake Tin

1 x No. 3 rectangular tin

Decorations

orange fruit sticks

6 blue sour straps

2 roll ups

2 coke bottles

2 plastic palm trees

2 cocktail umbrellas

2 small dolls

1 Preheat oven to 350°F (180°C) and butter and line the cake tin.

2 Prepare packets of cake mix, following directions on packet, and pour into the cake tin. Bake for 30 minutes, cover with foil and bake for another 45 minutes. Test with a skewer to make sure the cake is cooked. Leave to cool for 10 minutes, then turn onto a cooling rack.

3 Meanwhile, prepare the jelly according to the directions on the packet and refrigerate to set.

4 While cake cools, colour the frosting orange.

5 Use a serrated knife to level the cake. Using a palette knife, frost the cake. Cut the fruit sticks into thirds and assemble on the cake, forming a rectangle to make a pool. Line the inside of the pool with sour straps to stop the jelly from leaking. Spoon the jelly into the pool. Cut the edges of the roll ups to resemble towels. Use the remaining decorations to finish the cake.

lap pool

4 x 12oz (340g) packets butter cake mix

2 packets blue jelly

2 packets green jelly

½ quantity butter cream frosting (see page 9)

blue icing paste

Cake Tin

1 x No. 3 rectangular tin

Decorations

1 packet blue sour straps

2 candy necklaces

2 small dolls

1 Preheat oven to 350°F (180°C) and butter and line the cake tin.

2 Prepare packets of cake mix, following directions on packet, and pour into the cake tin. Bake for 30 minutes, cover with foil and bake for another 45 minutes. Test with a skewer to make sure the cake is cooked. Leave to cool for 10 minutes, then turn onto a cooling rack.

3 Meanwhile, prepare the jelly according to the directions on the packet and refrigerate to set.

4 While cakes cool, colour the frosting blue.

5 Use a serrated knife to level the cake. Using a palette knife, frost the cake. Cut out the top third of the cake, to make a pool. Cut the sour straps into squares and attach to outside of pool, as tiles. Spoon the blue and green jellies into the pool, then cut the candy necklaces to appropriate lengths and lay on top, as water and laneways. Finish by adding some swimmers.

fort fingers

6 x 12oz (340g) packets butter cake mix

1 quantity chocolate butter cream frosting (see page 9)

Cake Tin

1 x No. 4 rectangular tin

Decorations

3 packets chocolate finger biscuits

6 chocolate liquorice logs

plastic cowboy and Indians toys

4 flags (see Templates section)

1 banner (see Templates section)

1 Preheat oven to 350°F (180°C) and butter and line the cake tin.

2 Prepare packets of cake mix, following directions on packet, and pour into the cake tin. Bake for 60 minutes, cover with foil and bake for another 40 minutes. Test with a skewer to make sure the cake is cooked. Leave to cool for 10 minutes, then turn onto a cooling rack.

3 Use a ruler to divide cake into three even logs. Cut one log in half and leave the other two whole. Form the pieces into a square, with the two smaller pieces placed at either end of the two longer pieces, forming a square. Secure them with skewers and frosting.

4 Using a palette knife, frost the cake. Place the chocolate fingers around the outside of the cake. Cut 2 of the liquorice logs in half and place on each corner of the cake. Use the remaining decorations to finish the rest of the fort.

templates

Increase templates to 200%.

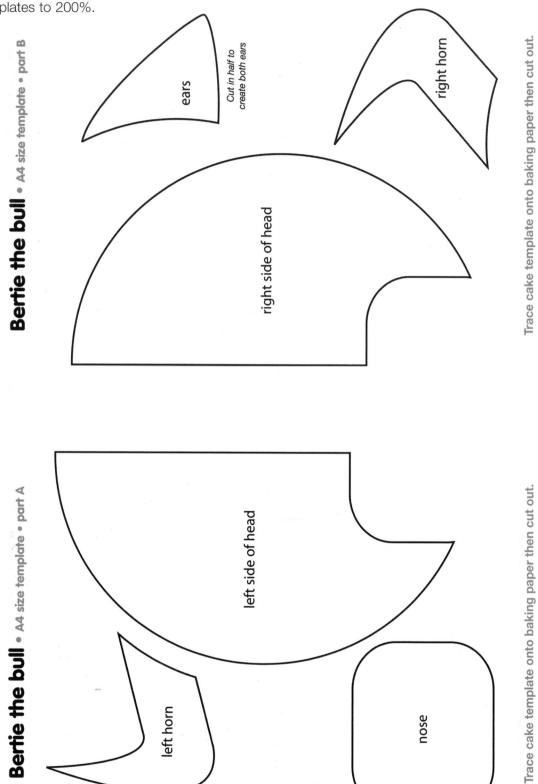

Bertie the bull • A4 size template • part B

ears

Cut in half to create both ears

right horn

right side of head

Trace cake template onto baking paper then cut out.

Bertie the bull • A4 size template • part A

left horn

left side of head

nose

Trace cake template onto baking paper then cut out.

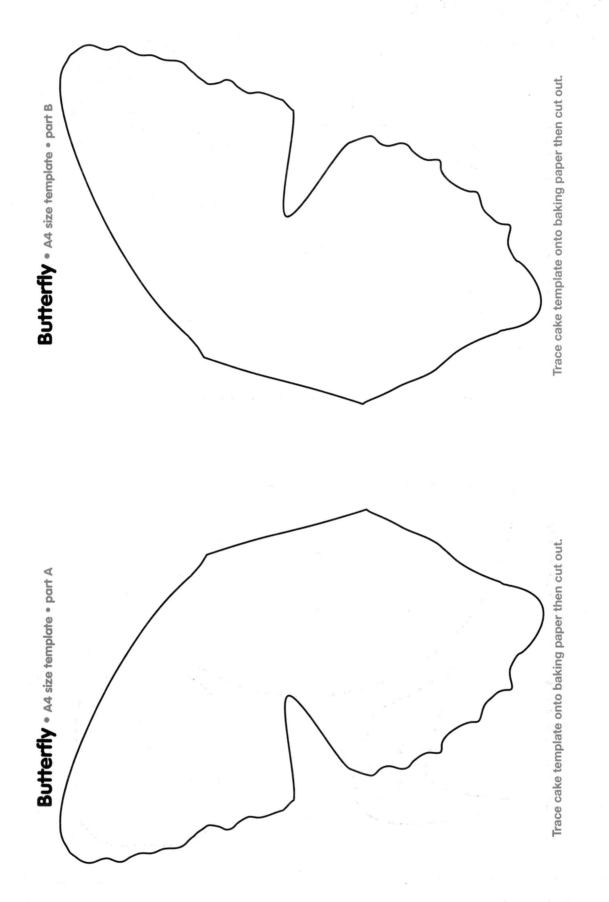

Butterfly • A4 size template • part B

Trace cake template onto baking paper then cut out.

Butterfly • A4 size template • part A

Trace cake template onto baking paper then cut out.

Trace cake template onto baking paper then cut out.

Butterfly • A4 size template • part C

Cut in half to create the other half of the butterfly

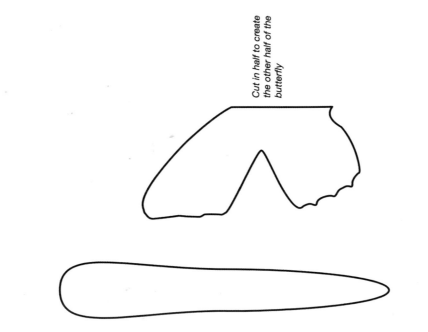

Trace cake template onto baking paper then cut out.

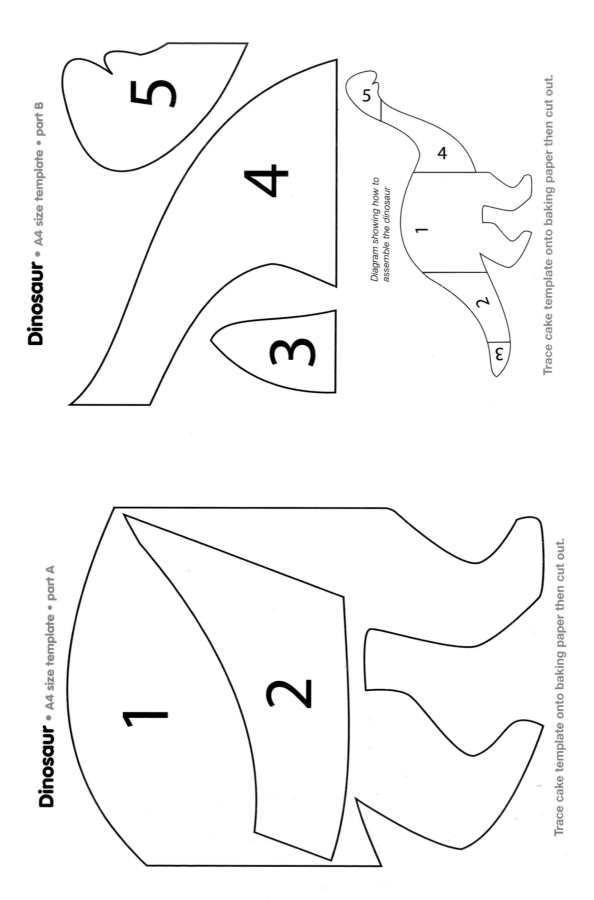

Dinosaur • A4 size template • part B

5

4

3

Diagram showing how to assemble the dinosaur

5

4

1

2

3

Trace cake template onto baking paper then cut out.

Dinosaur • A4 size template • part A

1

2

Trace cake template onto baking paper then cut out.

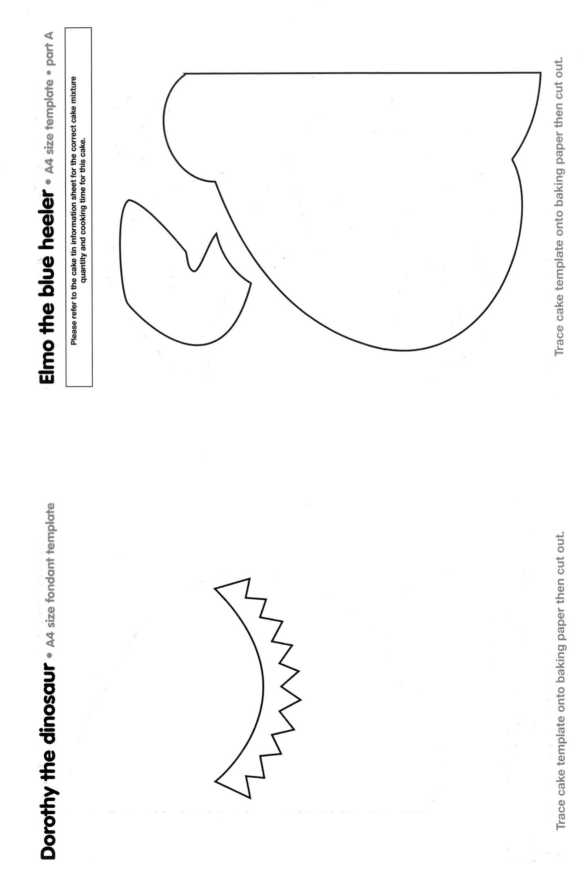

Elmo the blue heeler • A4 size template • part A

Please refer to the cake tin information sheet for the correct cake mixture quantity and cooking time for this cake.

Trace cake template onto baking paper then cut out.

Dorothy the dinosaur • A4 size fondant template

Trace cake template onto baking paper then cut out.

Elmo the blue heeler • A4 size fondant template

Eyes

Eye patch

Tongue

Nose

Trace cake template onto baking paper then cut out.

Elmo the blue heeler • A4 size template • part B

Please refer to the cake tin information sheet for the correct cake mixture quantity and cooking time for this cake.

Trace cake template onto baking paper then cut out.

Emily the elephant · A4 size template · part B

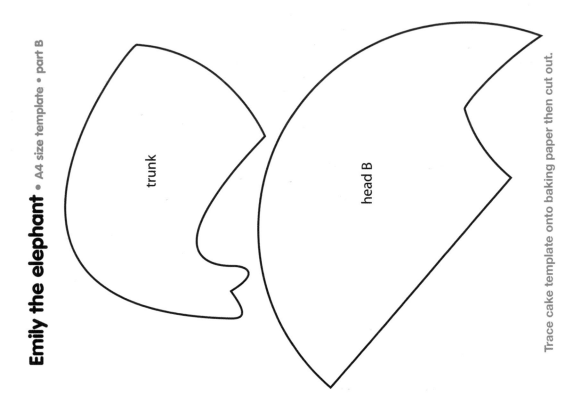

trunk

head B

Trace cake template onto baking paper then cut out.

Emily the elephant · A4 size template · part A

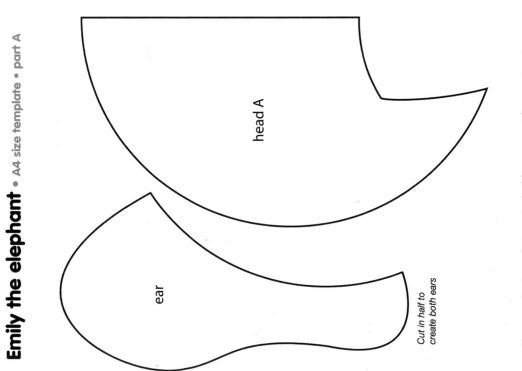

head A

ear

Cut in half to create both ears

Trace cake template onto baking paper then cut out.

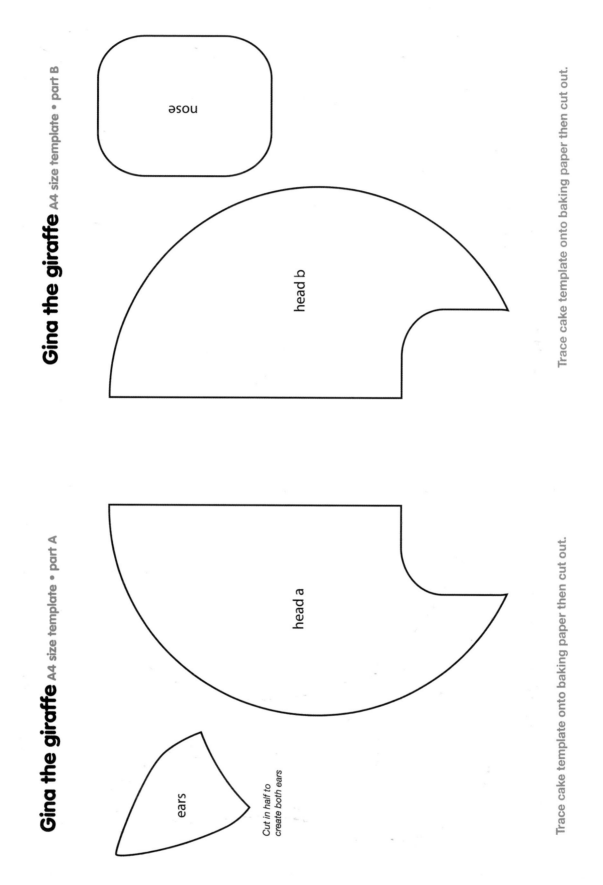

nose

head b

Trace cake template onto baking paper then cut out.

Gina the giraffe A4 size template • part A

head a

ears

*Cut in half to
create both ears*

Trace cake template onto baking paper then cut out.

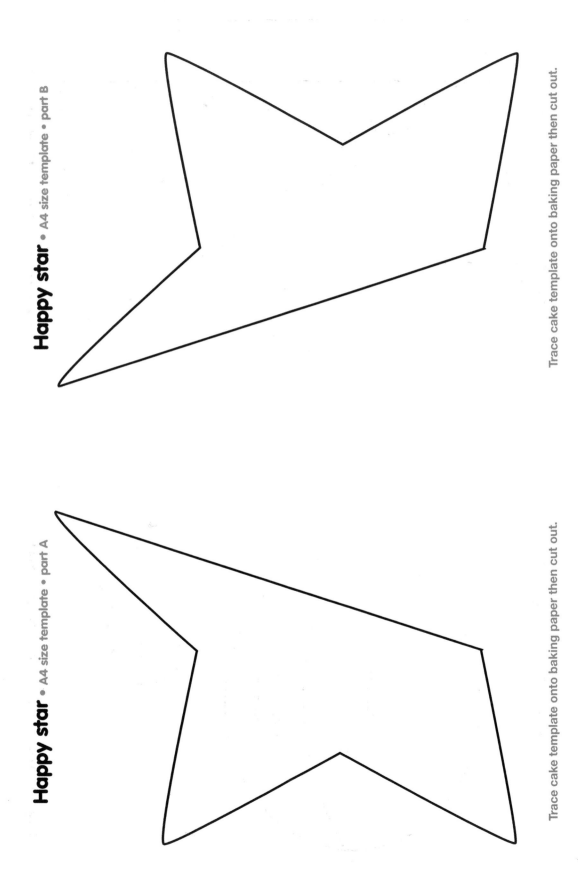

Happy star • A4 size template • part B

Trace cake template onto baking paper then cut out.

Happy star • A4 size template • part A

Trace cake template onto baking paper then cut out.

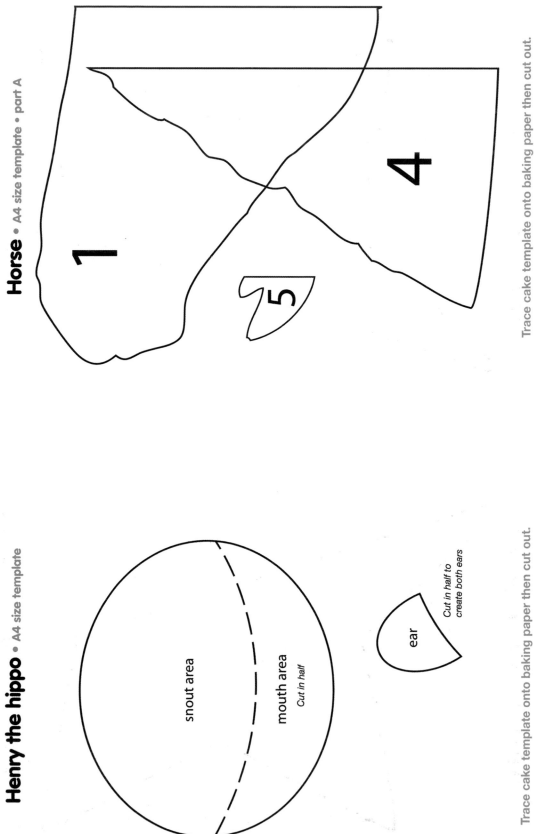

Horse • A4 size template • part A

1

4

5

Trace cake template onto baking paper then cut out.

Henry the hippo • A4 size template

snout area

mouth area
Cut in half

ear

*Cut in half to
create both ears*

Trace cake template onto baking paper then cut out.

Horse • A4 size template • part C

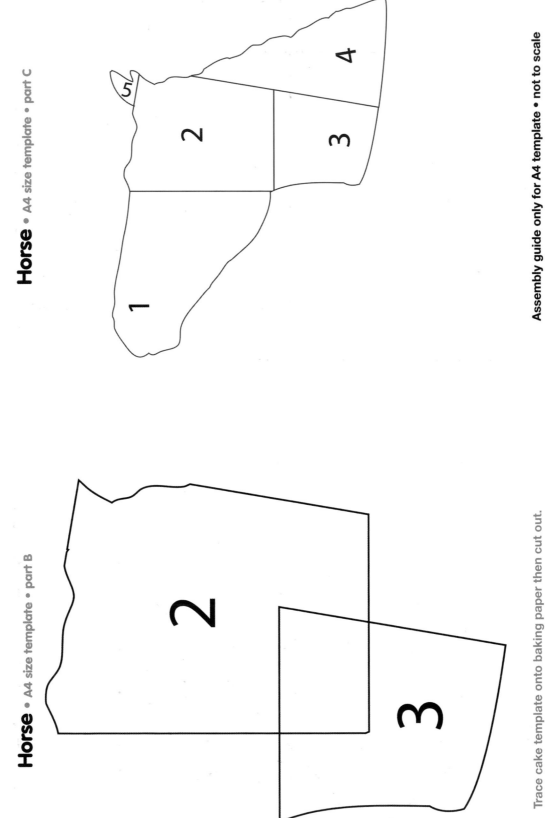

Assembly guide only for A4 template • not to scale

Horse • A4 size template • part B

Trace cake template onto baking paper then cut out.

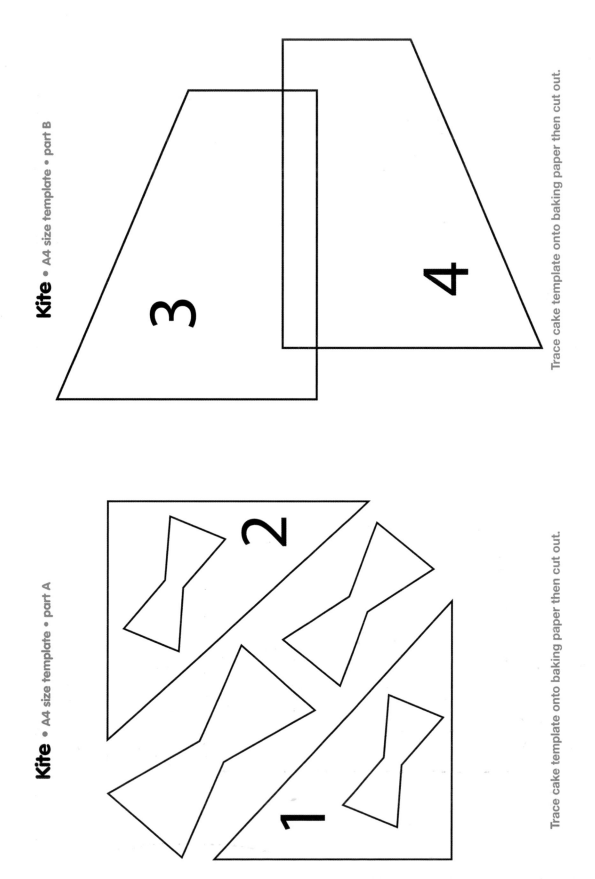

Kite • A4 size template • part B

Trace cake template onto baking paper then cut out.

3

4

Kite • A4 size template • part A

Trace cake template onto baking paper then cut out.

2

1

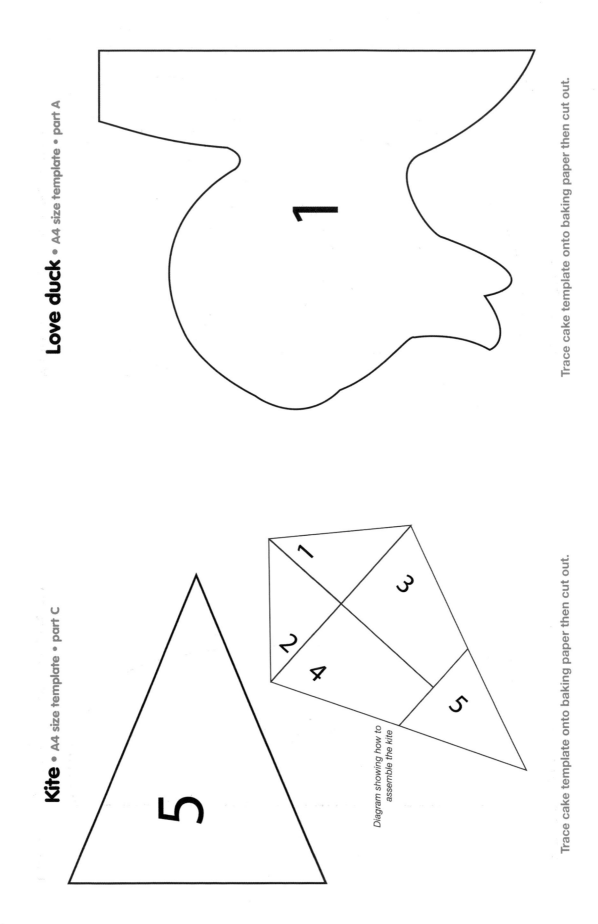

Love duck • A4 size template • part A

1

Trace cake template onto baking paper then cut out.

Kite • A4 size template • part C

5

1

3

2

4

5

Diagram showing how to assemble the kite

Trace cake template onto baking paper then cut out.

Love duck • A4 size template • part C

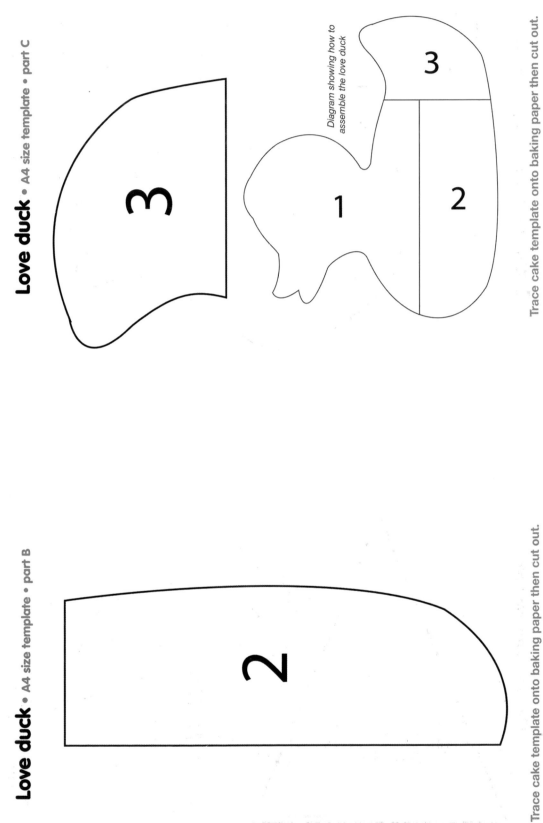

3

Diagram showing how to assemble the love duck

3

1

2

Trace cake template onto baking paper then cut out.

Love duck • A4 size template • part B

2

Trace cake template onto baking paper then cut out.

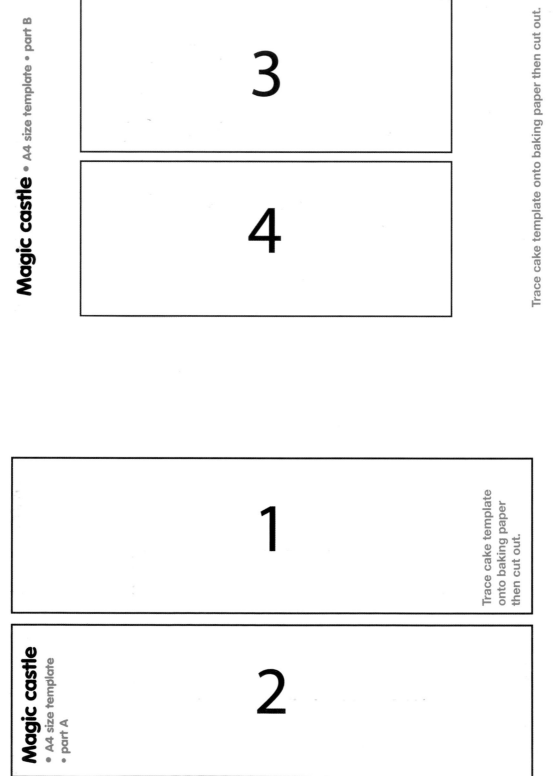

Magic castle • A4 size template • part B

3

4

Trace cake template onto baking paper then cut out.

1

Trace cake template onto baking paper then cut out.

Magic castle
• A4 size template
• part A

2

Mary the mouse • A4 size template

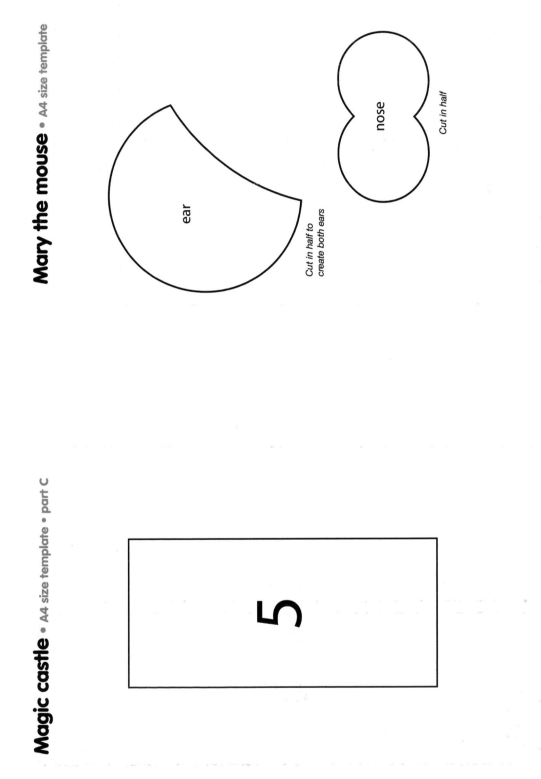

ear

Cut in half to create both ears

nose

Cut in half

Trace cake template onto baking paper then cut out.

Magic castle • A4 size template • part C

5

Trace cake template onto baking paper then cut out.

Moon • A4 size template

Please refer to the cake tin information sheet for the correct cake mixture quantity and cooking time for this cake.

Please note: This cake uses No. 3 rectangular tin: 275 x 225mm

Trace cake template onto baking paper then cut out.

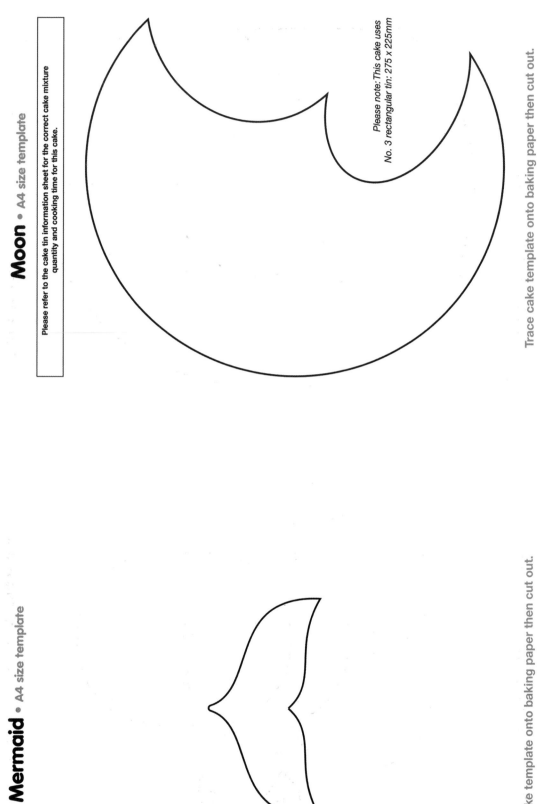

Mermaid • A4 size template

Trace cake template onto baking paper then cut out.

Number 2 • A4 size template • part A

Trace cake template onto baking paper then cut out.

Morris the monkey • A4 size template

eyes

nose and mouth

ear

Cut in half to create both ears

Trace cake template onto baking paper then cut out.

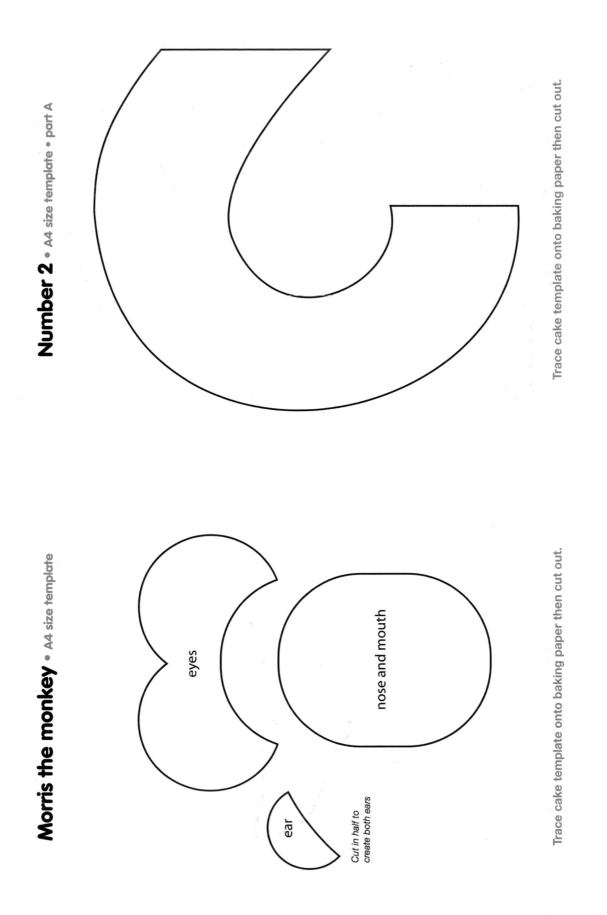

Number 4 • A4 size template • part A

Please refer to the cake tin information sheet for the correct cake mixture quantity and cooking time for this cake.

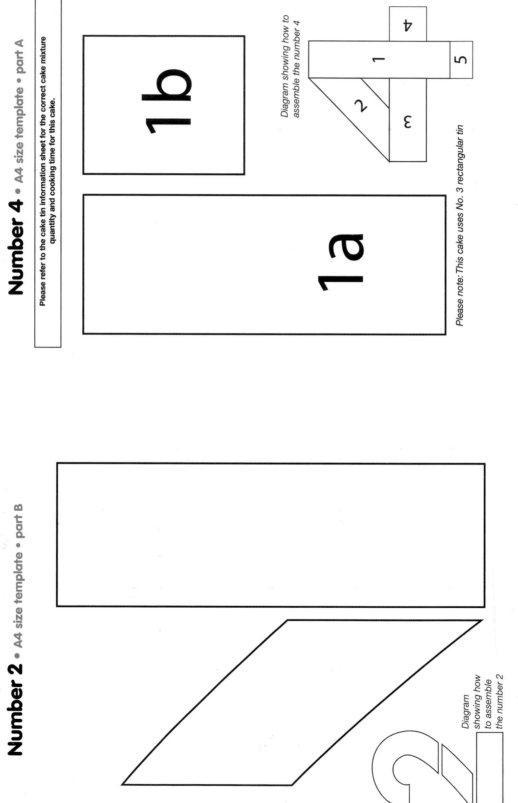

1b

1a

Diagram showing how to assemble the number 4

Please note: This cake uses No. 3 rectangular tin

Trace cake template onto baking paper then cut out.

Number 2 • A4 size template • part B

Diagram showing how to assemble the number 2

Trace cake template onto baking paper then cut out.

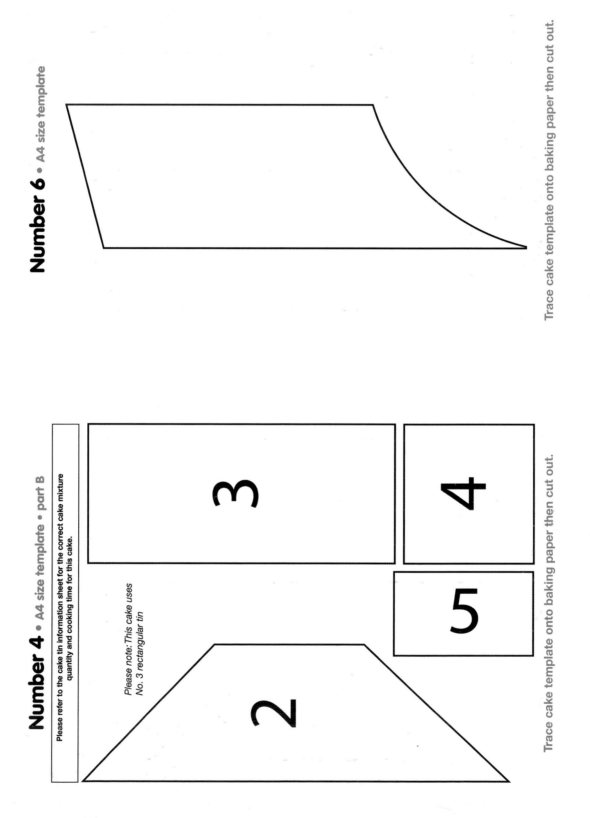

Number 6 • A4 size template

Trace cake template onto baking paper then cut out.

Number 4 • A4 size template • part B

Please refer to the cake tin information sheet for the correct cake mixture quantity and cooking time for this cake.

Please note: This cake uses No. 3 rectangular tin

3

4

5

2

Trace cake template onto baking paper then cut out.

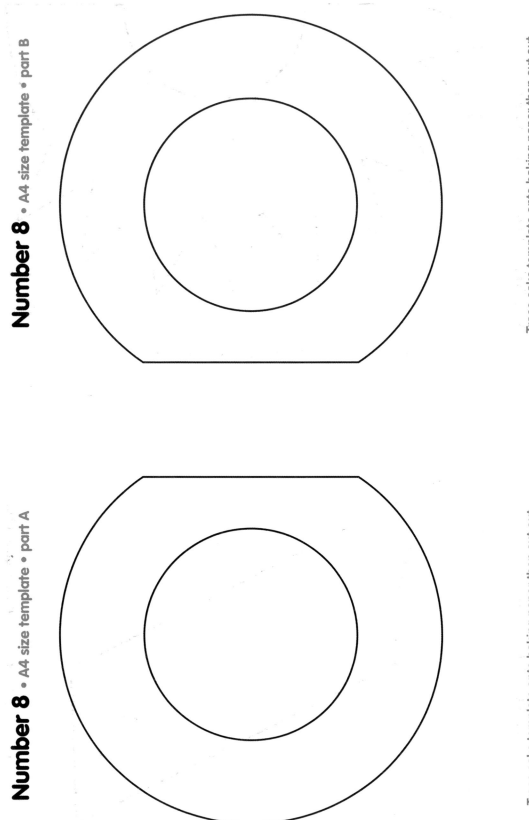

Number 8 • A4 size template • part B

Trace cake template onto baking paper then cut out.

Number 8 • A4 size template • part A

Trace cake template onto baking paper then cut out.

Number 9 • A4 size fondant template • part A

Trace cake template onto baking paper then cut out.

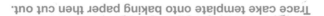

Number 9 • A4 size template

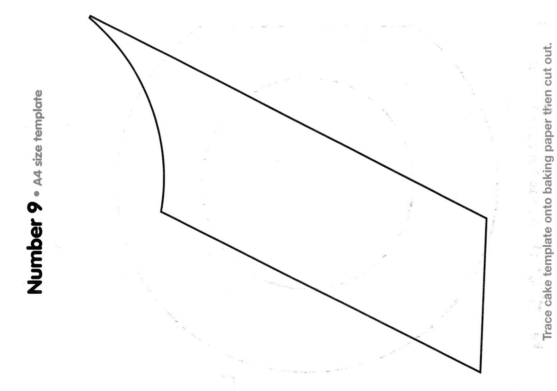

Trace cake template onto baking paper then cut out.

Penelope the pig • A4 size template

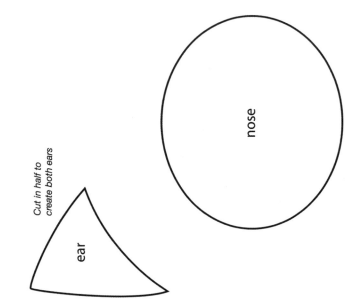

Cut in half to
create both ears

ear

nose

Trace cake template onto baking paper then cut out.

Trace cake template onto baking paper then cut out.

Number 9 • A4 size fondant template • part B

Polly the panda • A4 size template

ear

Cut in half to create both ears

snout

Trace cake template onto baking paper then cut out.

Rocket • A4 size template • part A

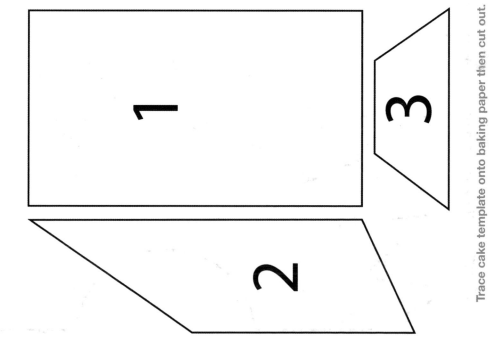

1

2

3

Trace cake template onto baking paper then cut out.

Rocket • A4 size template • part C

9

Trace cake template onto baking paper then cut out.

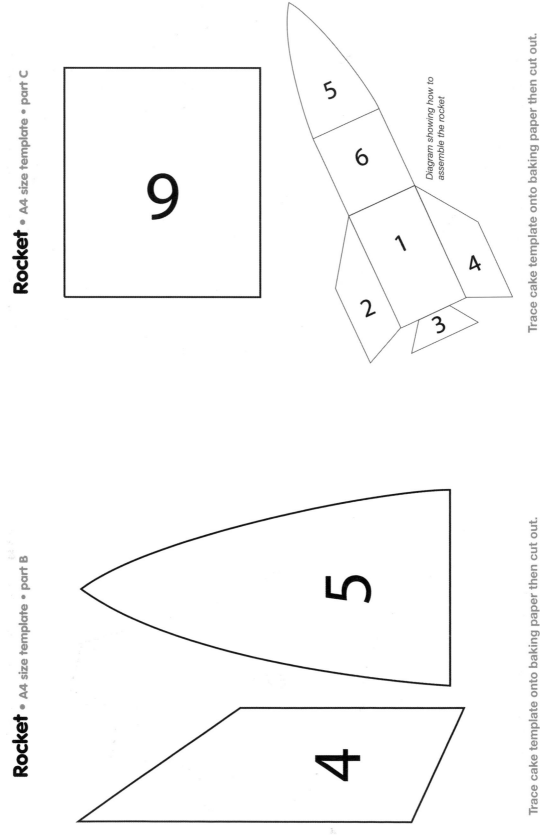

Diagram showing how to assemble the rocket

5

6

1

2

4

3

Rocket • A4 size template • part B

5

4

Trace cake template onto baking paper then cut out.

Seahorse • A4 size template • part B

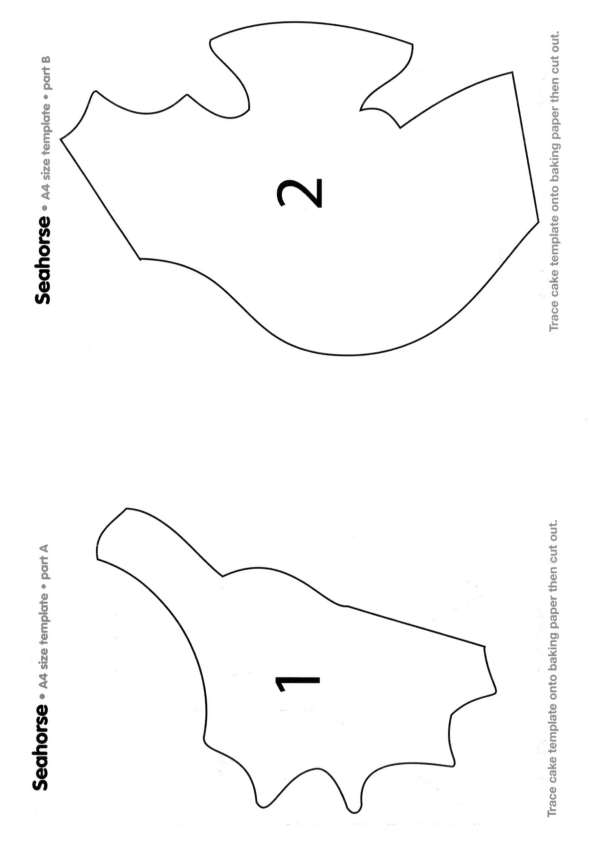

2

Trace cake template onto baking paper then cut out.

Seahorse • A4 size template • part A

1

Trace cake template onto baking paper then cut out.

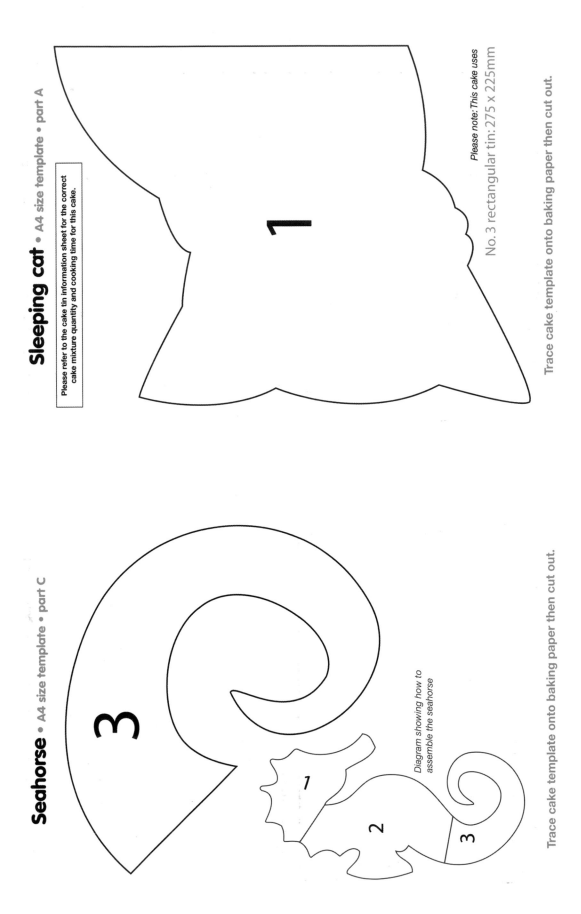

Sleeping cat • A4 size template • part A

Please refer to the cake tin information sheet for the correct cake mixture quantity and cooking time for this cake.

1

Please note: This cake uses
No. 3 rectangular tin: 275 x 225mm

Trace cake template onto baking paper then cut out.

Seahorse • A4 size template • part C

3

Diagram showing how to assemble the seahorse

1
2
3

Trace cake template onto baking paper then cut out.

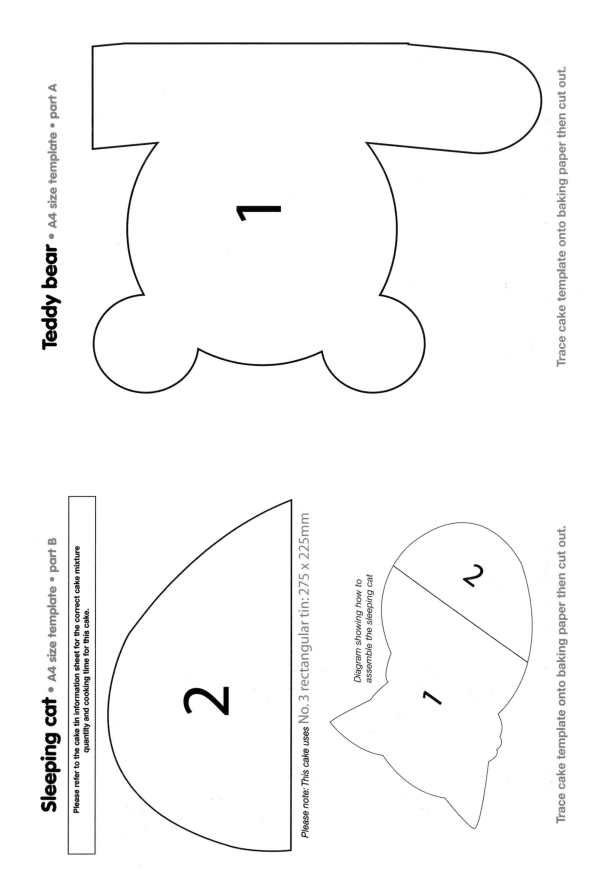

Teddy bear • A4 size template • part A

1

Trace cake template onto baking paper then cut out.

Sleeping cat • A4 size template • part B

Please refer to the cake tin information sheet for the correct cake mixture quantity and cooking time for this cake.

2

Please note: This cake uses No. 3 rectangular tin: 275 x 225mm

Diagram showing how to assemble the sleeping cat

2

1

Trace cake template onto baking paper then cut out.

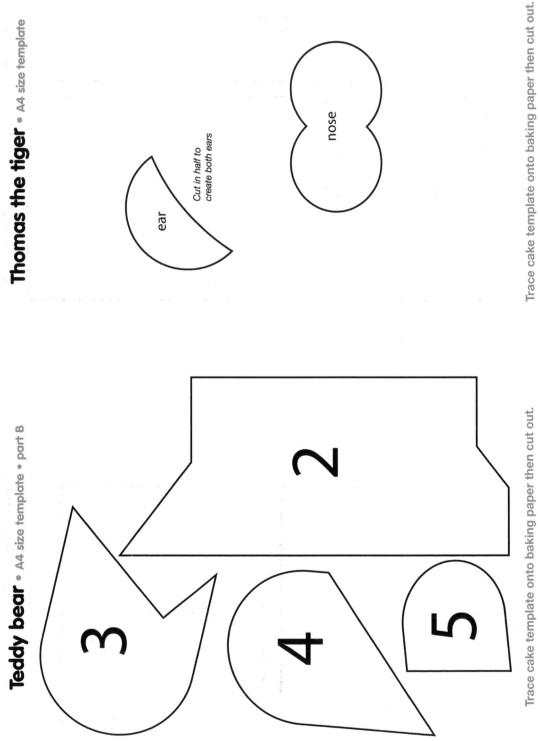

ear

Cut in half to
create both ears

nose

Trace cake template onto baking paper then cut out.

Teddy bear • A4 size template • part B

2

3

4

5

Trace cake template onto baking paper then cut out.

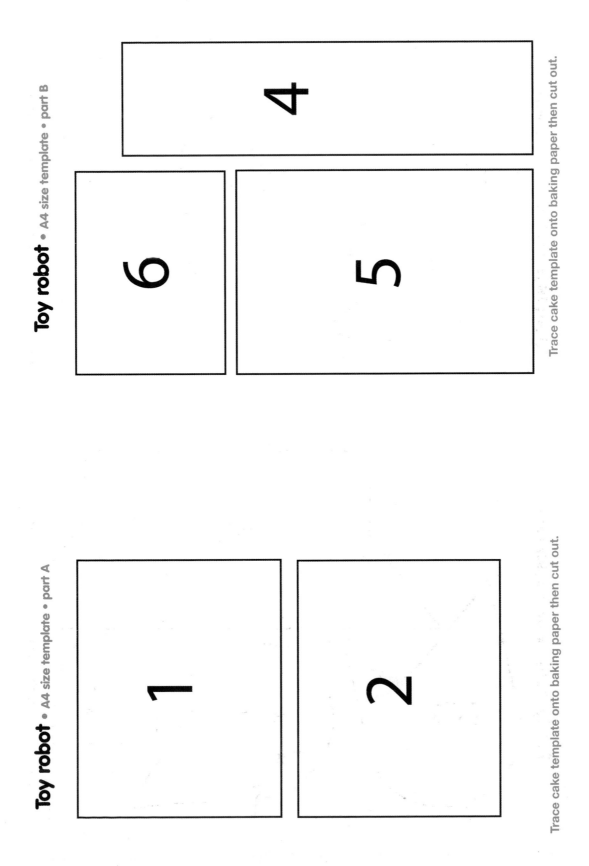

Toy robot • A4 size template • part B

4

6

5

Trace cake template onto baking paper then cut out.

Toy robot • A4 size template • part A

1

2

Trace cake template onto baking paper then cut out.

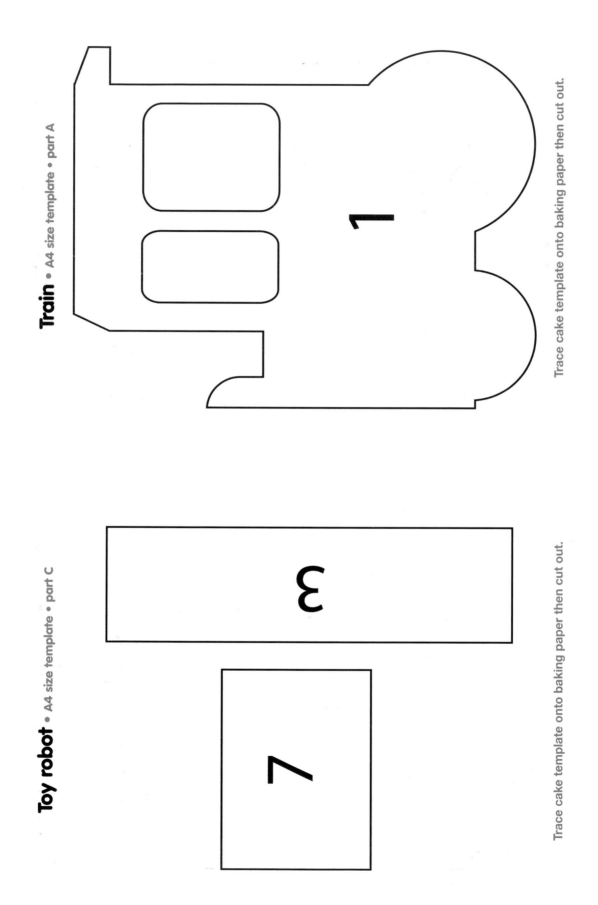

Train • A4 size template • part A

Trace cake template onto baking paper then cut out.

1

Toy robot • A4 size template • part C

Trace cake template onto baking paper then cut out.

3

7

Zephyr the zebra • A4 size template • part A

head a

ear

Cut in half to create both ears

mane

Trace cake template onto baking paper then cut out.

Train • A4 size template • part B

3

2

3

1

2

Diagram showing how to assemble the train

Trace cake template onto baking paper then cut out.

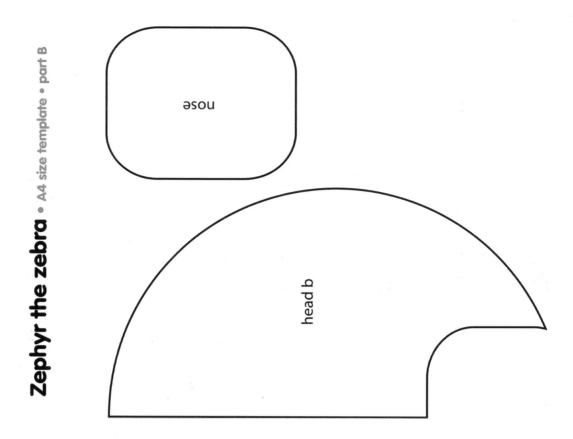

Cake tin information sheet

name	size	cake mixture quantity	cooking time
No. 1 rectangular tin	175 x 125mm	2 x 340g butter cake mix Use 2/3 of mix	40 minutes uncovered, plus 20 minutes covered
No. 2 rectangular tin	225 x 175mm	3 x 340g butter cake mix	35 minutes uncovered, plus 30 minutes covered
No. 3 rectangular tin	275 x 225mm	4 x 340g butter cake mix	50 minutes uncovered, plus 25 minutes covered
No. 4 rectangular tin	325 x 275mm	6 x 340g butter cake mix	60 minutes uncovered, plus 40 minutes covered
No. 1 bar tin	200 x 75 x 75mm	1 x 340g butter cake mix	50 minutes to cook
No. 2 bar tin	225 x 75 x 75mm	1 x 340g butter cake mix	50–55 minutes to cook
No. 3 bar tin	300 x 75 x 75mm	2 x 340g butter cake mix Use 3/4 of mix	70 minutes to cook
large Dolly Varden tin	195mm diameter x 55mm deep	2 x 340g butter cake mix	30 minutes uncovered, plus 30 minutes covered
Round	220mm	2 x 340g butter cake mix	30 minutes uncovered, plus 30 minutes covered

Fort fingers flags • A4 size template

Cut out flags and fold on the dotted line around a toothpick

Cut out the banner and fold both ends on the dotted line around a toothpick

Use a toothpick for the flag pole.

Astronaut flag • A4 size template

Cut out flag and fold on the dotted line around a toothpick

Use a toothpick for the flag pole.

Chequered flag • A4 size template

Cut out flag and fold on the dotted line around a toothpick

Use a toothpick for the flag pole.

Magic castle flags • A4 size template

Cut out flags and fold on the dotted line around a toothpick

Use a toothpick for the flag pole.

Finish line banner · A4 size template

Finish

Cut out the banner and fold both ends on the dotted line around a toothpick

Use a toothpick for the flag poles.

Skull & crossbone flag · A4 size template

Cut out flag and fold on the dotted line around a toothpick

Use a toothpick for the flag pole.

Index